Bushido

A Practical Guide to Living the Way of the Warrior

(A Journey to the Interior of a Warrior's Spirit The truth about Japanese Samurai wisdom)

Margret Richardson

Published By **Phil Dawson**

Margret Richardson

Bushido: A Practical Guide to Living the Way of the Warrior (A Journey to the Interior of a Warrior's Spirit The truth about Japanese Samurai wisdom)

ISBN 978-1-9995502-7-1

No part of this guidebook shall be reproduced in any form without permission in writing from the publisher except in the case of brief quotations embodied in critical articles or reviews.

Legal & Disclaimer

The information contained in this book is not designed to replace or take the place of any form of medicine or professional medical advice. The information in this book has been provided for educational & entertainment purposes only.

The information contained in this book has been compiled from sources deemed reliable, and it is accurate to the best of the Author's knowledge; however, the Author cannot guarantee its accuracy and validity and cannot be held liable for any errors or omissions. Changes are periodically made to this book. You must consult your doctor or get professional medical advice before using any of the suggested remedies, techniques, or information in this book.

Upon using the information contained in this book, you agree to hold harmless the Author from and against any damages, costs, and expenses, including any legal fees potentially resulting from the application of any of the information provided by this guide. This disclaimer applies to any damages or injury caused by the use and application, whether directly or indirectly, of any advice or information presented, whether for breach of contract, tort, negligence, personal injury, criminal intent, or under any other cause of action.

You agree to accept all risks of using the information presented inside this book. You need to consult a professional medical practitioner in order to ensure you are both able and healthy enough to participate in this program.

Table Of Contents

Chapter 1: The Path to Enlightenment

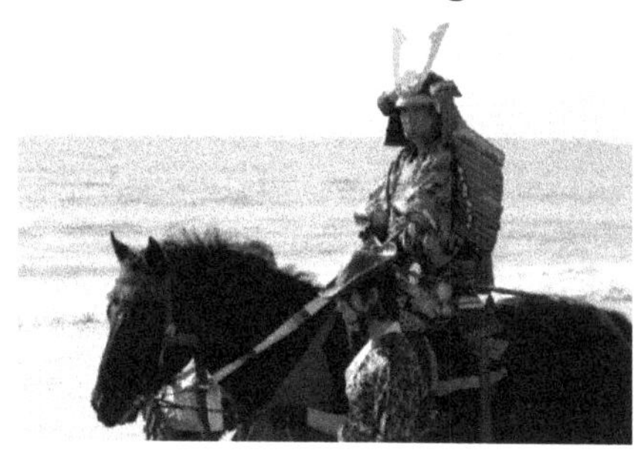

"Bushido as a code of conduct independent of conduct could vanish yet its influence won't be lost forever; its martial arts schools or honorable conduct could be destroyed, but the light and glory last for a long time after their demolishment. Much like the symbolism of a flowers, once it has been carried away to four directions and tossed to the four winds, it will continue to bless humanity with its fragrance the ability to enrich lives."

- InazoNitobe, Bushido: The Soul of Japan.

A Classic Essay on Samurai Ethics.

Bushido (Wu Shi Dao)) is an Japanese word (direct meaning: bu military;

Shi do - Knight, Do - Ways) that is loosely translated to mean The Way of the Warrior. In the past, it was referred to in The Japanese warrior Samurai code of behaviour. Today, for most individuals, Samurai means Japanese warrior. It's not completely wrong but does obscure what Samurai really means.

character of the Samurai. In Japanese, Samurai

(Shi

Actually means"To

Serve". It is not a Way of Violence, but of Service.

It is however not the sole code of conduct that has be found in the history of mankind. It is also The Chivalry Code Of Conduct that was used by knights from

Europe in addition to the Spartan Code of Honor - invented by the famous brave warriors of the past which had codes that included a statute that prohibited to retreat from combat. These codes all have an appeal of their own, however they don't feature in the present book.

The Way of The Samurai is fairly well-known in comparison to other warrior codes that exist because of its use in self-obliteration (Seppuku)(Qie Fu) as well as the notion of honor being more significant over all other things.

life. Also, it has garnered a lot of interest in recent years because of its representation in Hollywood films such as The Last Samuraior 47 Ronin as well as The Last Samuraior 47 Ronin which has Bushido being the primary motif of both films.

Then, what exactly has this got in relation to our daily lives?

We should begin by examining the concept of Warrior. Do you consider yourself a warrior? The definition of warrior means "a person engaged in some struggle or conflict", i.e. one that FIGHTS.By the definition above, we all are fighters. If it's against hunger, poverty and illness... as well lesser physical challenges such as racism, discrimination, lack of significance, we are a part of every day fighting. as warriors. In case you didn't thought of it before that you're an armed warrior. Life isn't a solitary thing no matter if you're a or woman, young or adult from the struggles. Therefore, you require an army's guide that will guide you on how to live your life and fight... this is if you'd like to become a successful warrior. If you're looking to win. Do you really want to win, in the end? What better way to leverage the knowledge and experience of those who been on the same path as us?

What is the meaning of Way? What would be the Way? How do you achieve success? The best way to earn some money? It is not, but the word Way is a reference to ethical principles in life as a means of adhering to a certain code of conduct. Therefore you can say that the Bushido could be described as the principle of life for an individual warrior, the way for living in harmony. As we all are fighters of our own The Bushido can be our way and guideline in each battle. This is the goal of this book and that's to provide you with an introduction to the code of ancient wisdom that is Bushido as well as to draw you on the advantages using the principles and knowledge of Bushido in your daily life and the battles you fight.

In the book, you'll find quotes from Samurai who have traveled the Way prior to us along with quotes the work of InazoNitobe, Dr. InazoNitobe, who deserves an extra mention for his authoritative study of the Bushido code in Bushido the Soul of Japan, which has brought numerous (including the author) to better understand the meaning of Bushido.

The work of Dr.Inazo has been around for 100 years The author was inspired by Dr. Inazo's work and had the desire to teach others an updated version of Bushido. The result was the creation of the following book: Bushido The Place Where Honor is stronger than Steel.

Are you prepared? Let's go in search of the Way all together.

Yi

(gi)

Righteousness

"Rectitude is one's power to decide upon a course of conduct in accordance with reason, without wavering; to die when to die is right, to strike when to strike is right."

- Anonymous Japanese Samurai

There are eight main concepts of Bushido which are known as Eight Virtues of Bushido. Some readers might be surprised and those who's perception about the Samurai is of a militaristic or combative type, but the most fundamental principle in Bushido is the pursuit of righteousness. It is not courage, but the Samurai were fearless, bordering of recklessness. It was not loyalty, even though the Samurai was a believer in loyalty to the end of time.

But the primary principle which a warrior must be taught from the Bushido Code, is righteousness. Justice. It is the rightness of a motive. It is not a reference to self-righteousness in which someone believes that they are better than others. It is the conviction in justice, and the determination to be a good person under all conditions.

Consider this for a second. The Samurai thought that righteousness was the base of Bushido as the basis of the Way. It was also considered to be the very first step in the path. Why did they choose righteousness as their initial stage?

Take a look at the alternative: if the basis of the Way of warriors was strength and determination, shouldn't the Way be based on the conviction the belief that "Might is Right" ? Then if the underlying principle of the Way was the concept of loyalty... shouldn't the Way be a sign of loyalty to an evil ruler?

In fact, the history of mankind has plenty of instances of brave warriors who pledged their allegiance to rulers who were evil and, as a result of they endorsed and promoted wickedness, since the foundation of their ethos was loyalty, not righteousness.

The concept of righteousness as the foundation of Bushido is that an Samurai needs to consider and determine if it's RIGHTto take his sword before swinging the sword. The reason he does not fight is for the sake of being the most powerful warrior. Nor is he fighting for the sake of being told to fight. He fights simply because it's right for him to fight.

This indicates that the Samurai knew the consequences of their actions and their potential consequences. If you're about to fight that could result in death of a person It is not necessary to think about whether the death is required or if it can be prevented? Prior to strength, prior to ability the concept of righteousness should be considered at first. It is the very first idea that comes to mind of a Samurai.

The Samurai is honest and open with other people and adheres to justice as a concept. Moral judgments aren't made with shades of gray, they are only right and wrong.

"All men's souls are immortal, but the souls of the righteous are immortal and divine."

-

Bertrand Russell

Righteousness is fortunately not yet an "old-fashioned" idea; in fact, it is still relevant and very much needed in today's society.Injustice is still a common occurrenceeverywhere, be it schools, workplaces, on the streets.

There are two elements of righteousness that are certainly needed in our life. The first is the desire to follow the right path and to take the right decision. A second is determination to speak out against things that are Wrong and stop the injustices from taking place.

If you are involved in any personal battles, be sure you're fighting on your right side. This is not about the more powerful side and, more accurately and on the right side. Believing that you're taking the proper path can give you a feeling of confidence and an absence of doubt.

Can you discern? Well, that's easy. If you're not certain what side is the right one, why do you fighting? It is only appropriate to "draw your sword" once you've analyzed and determined that it's appropriate to act accordingly.

Conflict at work will always happen; disputes are inevitable in the event of at least two employees working together.

Employers, you should not engage in fights or be caught up in fighting if you don't know which is the best or worst one. It's better not to even bother to pick fights initially. Therefore, please do avoid getting involved in a fight when you are unable to determine who is on the best position.

It's less about taking care of your own business, and it's more about doing the right What. If you want to do what is right is to know the issue first. Do not get involved in a dispute with your boss unless know that your job is sound and you're doing the right thing.

What about in a corporate situation? This is the similar: ensure that the decision you make is founded upon righteousness and not driven by greed or fear. Don't put a premium on getting a quick profit and it's rarely the best (or the most lucrative) decision. Avoid making business deals that involve dishonest or unreliable business all regardless of how great the deal seems to be. It is likely that the offer that appears too appealing to be true is it's actually too good to be true.

An unwise decision could lead to massive losses from your side. To prevent (or substantially decrease) the chance of this being the case Why not take a moment and take your time thinking it over?

In essence, you need to ensure you're making good selections, and for the correct reason... That's the only thing you require!

Chapter 2: Yong

(yu)

Heroic Courage

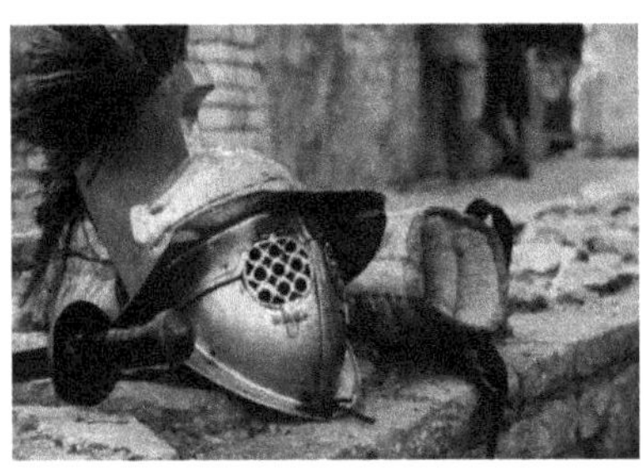

"Perceiving what is right and doing it not reveals a lack of Courage"

- Confucius

The form of courage that is spoken on within the Bushido code isn't much different from the types of courage described in western wisdom texts. It is however different because it is more tightly linked to the pursuit of righteousness. If righteousness involves making the right choice, it is necessary to have courage to take action on the decision.

An empathetic man could defend himself against ten people or even have the courage to venture into mountain ranges and forests alone. True courage, however, is shown when a weak person takes on a tough opponent and asks the bully to put down his weapons. The true test of courage occurs by a person who is afraid of water, leaps into the ocean to save an individual.

According to the Samurai the amount of bravery in a warrior cannot be measured solely by the ability to hold a sword, but rather by the level of fearlessness and the ability to fight. In fact the Samurai believed that courage was an attribute that is inextricably linked to determination of the mind or fortitude in the spirits.

The concept of courage, especially for warriors could appear to be a straightforward idea - look at the enemy take your sword, and confront the opponent. As mentioned yet again, the concept of bravery is a key element in Bushido is very closely linked to the virtues. So, with that thought in mind the Samurai must consider all the aspects before deciding which path to take then the Samurai must summon his strength.

It was once the case that there was a samurai named MusashiboBenkei(Wu Zang Fang Bian Qing . He was

An orthodox warrior monk of the 12th century who was famous for his incredible power. It was reported that he overcome more than 1000 people, in duel as well as in combat. But, that's not why he's famous. Benkei is known for his "holding the bridge" incident at Koromogawa no

Tate castle. So that he could give his master Minamoto not to be a slave.

Yoshitsune(Yuan Yi Jing), time to commit seppuku), Benkei played the lead

bridge that was in the front of the main gate alone against the army of the enemy, and the bridge was where he killed a staggering 300 of the enemy troops. According to legend, the troops of the enemy were scared of facing Benkei during close combat that they decided to kill and shoot Benkei using bows. So, it is not Benkei's power or ability that has been praised until the present day, but rather is his resolve to hold and defend his master until the end and his determination to face the entire enemy force on his own.

A Samurai does not hesitate to take action in the name of the righteous and in defending justice.

"I realized that courage was not just the absence of fear rather, the victory over it. A brave person isn't the one who isn't fearful, but rather one who overcomes anxiety."

- Nelson Mandela

In the same way as the virtue of being right, courage hasn't been a thing of the past today in the world of. The movies of superheroes like Superman or Batman in which the protagonist has the courage to stand up for the wrong, are highly sought-after. Also, we encounter situations every day that might not be as thrilling in comparison to movies about superheroes yet require courage nonetheless.

Don't confuse the concept of courage with traditional courage. Someone who is courageous might choose to take part in an office meeting to present an innovative idea to management. A person who is courageous however will not be afraid to inform the manager in a candid manner that the million-dollar venture currently in progress is unlikely to succeeding, regardless of the fact that the idea was recommended by the manager in charge whom is well-known to be averse to negative criticism. He also holds grudges.

When it comes to business It isn't enough to just say "I will bravely take the risk in order to make money". The right business choice can result in short-term difficulties or losses; it is tempting to pursue the quick and easy route that requires that you give up your values or make use of unethical techniques. The most important factor here is the courage. It is the courage to accept the losses, instead of to cheat. It is the courage to honour the terms of contract even if that means your company's cash flow will be affected.

In order to have something worth having, you has to pay the cost; The price is determination to do what's the right thing to do. If every right choice brought wealth and ease so why should we have the courage to do so? The self-interest of the individual is enough. Therefore, if you want to be a brave fighter in our modern times take the correct decisions and fight bravely in your battles.

Ren

(jin)

Benevolence

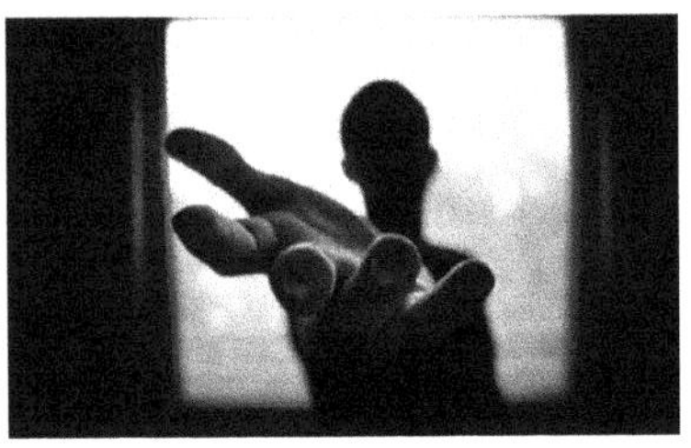

"The feeling of distress is the root of benevolence, therefore a benevolent man is ever mindful of those who are suffering and in distress."

- Mencius

The 3rd most significant characteristic that is mentioned as the third most important virtue in the Bushido code of conduct is kindness or compassion. It is a way to counterbalance the brutality of Samurai's responsibilities. Because the Samurai can kill anyone in his own life, he had to balance his heavy duties by showing compassion, kindness and mercy. This concept has its origins in Buddhism and is a way of teaching tolerance and compassion everyday life.

The Samurai is not supposed to have the heart of rage or hatred, but instead, an inner compassion to those in need as well as the vulnerable. Thus it is that a Samurai uses his sword to defend the weak because they're unable to defend them.

The same kind of generosity is extended to those who are the people they compete with The typical Samurai does not harbor anger or resentment against an other Samurai in battle. In combat, every Samurai will fight to the Bushido code of conduct, every one having faith in the cause of their respective and even laying down their life. But, this fighting was not restricted to only the battlefield and they were expected to show respect towards enemy warriors outside the battleground. They could acknowledge their fight for various motives, yet be aware that their adversaries were too adherents of Bushido who were fighting under the law of.

This is an illustration of kindness in the tale of UesugiKenshin.

(Shang Shan

Qian Xin) Qian Xin, Lord of Qian Xin), the Lord of Uesugi In the way he dealt with his foe Takeda

Shingen(Wu Tian Xin Xuan), Lord of the Takeda. The Takeda provinces are part of the Takeda

Clan was located in a mountainous area removed from the ocean, and was dependent on the Hojo provinces in the Tokaido to get salt. The Hojo sought to undermine Shingen's power, while refraining from openly fighting Shingen. Therefore, they removed all supply of salt that came from their Takeda clan. Kenshin was shocked to learn of the situation of his adversaries and the situation, informed Shingen that he believed Shingen was right. Hojo was guilty of committing a shady move, and also that even though Shingen (Kenshin) was in war with Shingen (Shingen) Shingen had already ordered his followers to supply his with salt. He also wrote that "I do not fight with salt, but with the sword".

A Samurai seeks out every chance to assist others, and also can create opportunities even when the opportunity does not appear.

"Kindness is a language the deaf can hear and the blind can see."

- Mark Twain

The world continues to be filled with the poor and vulnerable. A lot of people are in desperate need of mercy and compassion. If you're seeing a pattern this time, it's because the values that are found within the Bushido code remain essential in our current modern society.

The swords we wield may not be in use no more, and neither are we facing the problems due to the ravaging Mongols However, we do combat the tough battles though perhaps in a alternative setting. We are still afflicted by the iron feet of oppressors and exploiters.

Thus, compassion, kindness and kindness are required. If you're tough and have the strength to help those who are vulnerable. An wise man once stated "Those who have two coats, give one to those who have none". In Bushido the phrase is "With great power, show benevolence". It's a straightforward one, doesn't it? Give a helping hand. In the case of Samurai offer a sword in the event that it is appropriate. Show compassion to those that are less fortunate.

If you're in the business world, take into consideration your employees' needs as well as business associates. Everybody goes through tough times. Don't take advantage of those instances, instead try to offer an aid. If you are a business associate or vendor has trouble meeting their deadlines Do not revoke the agreement and take the full amount of meat from them as penalty. Be compassionate. It is likely that people will recall actions of kindness regardless of how little. It is possible that you might say that every bit of kindness you show to others will repay the person who helped you at some point in the future.

There are numerous current role models, who could be considered to be exemplary of kindness - it's easy to locate one to study from. There are numerous groups that focus on charity and kindness and volunteer groups and charities, for example. It's a small step, a single decision or a few minutes or so of time. A single choice that can make an impact on the lives of someone who is less fortunate and you'll be just one step away from living your Bushido lifestyle.

Li

(rei)

Respect

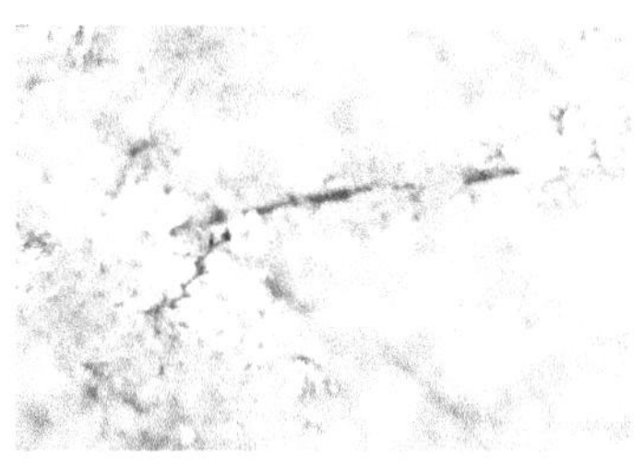

"When you are polite, the others think they are wearing flowers."

- Japanese proverb

The Bushido base of respect is honesty. Respect in the context of the Bushido code, is more than being able to say "please" and "thank you" In their eyes it's a genuine love to others from the inside that is reflected the same in their actions and speech.

To for a Samurai (and in the case of Japanese and even today) Respect does not only come from the language one uses but also by the manner in which they stand as well as the length of their bows, as well as other ways to honor the other. Even they have the "polite" form of the spoken language, which is more formal as opposed to "conversational" Japanese.

There's a good chance that you've watched comedies that show two Japanese bowing at each other frequently, and neither being leaving since they both believe they're the last to bow. This is a ploy for comedy purposes, however reality isn't as far from the truth.

From an "common sense" point of the world, being respectful and polite to another warrior is a lot of sense. After all, there's not much gain from being cut or cut due to offending someone on accidental. Therefore, Samurai bow whenever they see with one another, and they meet each other with respect. They are not known for their profane language, and don't try to offend or provoke fights.

The Samurai was a believer in respect for others such that they even had classes in etiquette as well as proper conduct. The most well-known school in

Etiquette, Ogasawara-ryu (Xiao Li Yuan Liu) is a famous saying:

"The end of all etiquette is to so cultivate your mind that even when you are quietly seated, not the roughest ruffian can dare make onset on your person." Imagine a degree of politeness that could be demonstrated by simply sitting in a quiet place with no words. What is the best way to behave politely? Should politeness be applied to standing or sitting? It is believed that the Samurai believed it did.

The Samurai does not have a reason to show cruelty nor is there any need to show his strength. The manner of conduct and respect that the Samurai from a wolf and shows the true strength of a person.

"Respect your fellow human beings' feelings. They may mean nothing to you but it might mean everything for them"

- Roy T. Bennett

It seems that our society today not have an understanding of respect, especially the young generation. Indeed, I'm pretty sure that we've all had to deal with rude people at some point during our lifetimes somewhere. You'll see it on the streets, at the workplace, and at the eateries we eat at and we're all too familiar with these kinds of things.

The people of today are becoming increasingly impatient and rude in their actions and words in general, with no consideration of the feelings of others. A attitude of disrespect for individuals and authorities is so widespread that we've gotten used to it or to it. It seems that we have too much emphasis on respect for ourselves and have a tendency to forget that we've forgotten the respect of others, especially to those who need respect the most.

There's nothing wrong with showing respect, kindness and the bare minimum of respect towards the people around you. Naturally, the level of respect will vary from one person to the next and there's nothing wrong with granting the highest amount of respect to those whose ideals and values are admirable and whom you look up to.

Take note of those in your vicinity. Be attentive to others' views and thoughts, and then encourage the person to share their ideas regardless of whether you are in agreement with them or you do not. Recognize the effort of others and express your gratitude and appreciation where it is appropriate.

In the business world, respect is a crucial factor ; your actions and words can possibly make or break the success of a multi-million dollar business. Do you really want to risk loss of money due to the carelessness of your remarks? The Japanese know respect well during business gatherings the Japanese businessperson will select his words with great diligence and won't choose the topics that may potentially cause an offense. There is a chance that we won't have the ability to influence additional factors that impact the deal such as the economy or exchange rate, but we are able to control the manner in which we conduct ourselves and our words.

In the workplace, how do you handle it? The importance of respect is just as crucial. It's not just for the bosses and supervisors you work with however, but to your colleagues and colleagues as well. Each of your coworkers is a professional with skills and experience that can help you or contribute to your job. In addition they are able to hold up or even create problems to your job when you do not respect their opinion. What do you get by doing something rude? Satisfaction? Worth the hassle you'll get?

Be respectful of others can not only assist your build a stronger relationship with your coworkers and friends, but it will also assist you over time. Your colleagues could be able to assist with issues to come across in the future.

Chapter 3: Cheng

(makoto)

Integrity

"It takes three years to learn to be a man of integrity; it only takes three days to degrade."

- Chinese Proverb

Integrity. Honesty. Sincerity. The words convey a sense that of stability and of someone who is able to stand up for his beliefs This is a crucial quality that any soldier should be able to. An honest person is able to speak the truth and to never lose your trust and not violate their principles A person whose word is solid as as steel.

Integrity was a constant concern for the Samurai. The Samurai considered it to be cowardly to deceive or lie and the Samurai thought the virtues of integrity and courage to be inseparable. The notion of lying was one of weak character and heart.

Like the French concept of Noblesse Olige as well, the Samurai considered that their status as a social elite was a requirement for them to maintain to be more honest as compared to the average citizen. This idea is prevalent in governments and the rulers of the world today but unfortunately, most respect this only for their comfort.

In situations where lives are on the line the warrior must to fulfill both roles: one who is assured of saying what he is saying and a soldier that can be trusted to follow through with what he has said.

The warrior could be charged to carry out important tasks and the outcome of battles or wars rest. When a bridge has to be maintained for two days in order to defeat enemies, or your troops are required to be forced-marching for a period of 2 days in order to get there on time... It is why you should look for an experienced warrior who can be assured that he will do the job the man says he'll perform.

Ask yourself, do you think this is integrity or reliable? These aren't two different things is it? It is my opinion that these two principles differ, however for Samurai, they were Samurai they were completely inseparable. In the eyes of an Samurai it is a sign of his strength that his word is believed to be reliable is testimony to his honesty and his faith in his relationship with the world.

It's a matter of pride to know that his honesty ensures his reliability to the death. If you had to confess the truth to save yourself, Would you? Would you tell someone when faced with the possibility of death "My vows are my pledge. What is it worth should I breach it in order in order to make my life better?"

A Samurai's conscience serves as the one who decides his honour. the decisions he takes and the way he carry his actions are reflections of his character. Make the right choice and without any hesitation.

"With integrity you will do the right thing, so you will have no guilt."

- ZigZiglar

Honesty is the only way to go A phrase most of us grew in hearing from our teachers and parents usually after an event or two in which we've perhaps not being as honest as we ought to have.

After having been through numerous occasions as well as incidents that which required honesty from you, or the insincerity from other people, what conclusion did you reached? Are honesty and integrity the right practice?

Integrity is among the top qualities that employers seek in their workers in the present. Only the most brave and trusted employees could put on their resumes "Character traits - Integrity, reliability, honesty". I am sure that this kind of candidate will be selected to be interviewed, and even hired in the event that they met the qualities listed in their resume.

I'll tell you that a trustworthy employee is worth every penny - no matter what the amount you pay them doesn't suffice. What's the best way to assign an amount on their the integrity of your employees? Are you able to determine if it is priceless because it cannot be bought using money? I've heard some employers claim "That is what I pay them for, it is only normal" These employers are either in denial or are ignorant. If you believe that giving anyone a few hundred dollars each month could assure reliability; consider that your employee isn't going to betray you, or do what you want, or will perform whatever it is they are required to do in exchange for the small amount you give you... and I predict some tough futures for you. That's why I'm repeating that integrity as a character quality in a person is invaluable. A person who is given a million dollars the bag and relied on to carry this bag to the bank without ever looking within, is an employee with the character that of an enigmatic Samurai.

The same is true when it comes to business. The integrity of a businessperson is known in the marketplace - no one is hesitant to conduct business with him. Nobody would doubt the authenticity of his claims. If a businessman claims that the venture will bring an ROI of 500 percent, nobody doubts that he is exaggerating or manipulating the numbers.

A businessman is never short of partners or investors, and will always able to get loans. How much would businesspeople spend to have such confidence, the ease with which they conduct dealing? It is possible that I am repetitious, but I can't be more clear that honesty is an investment. It's not available for purchase. It is only earned and demonstrated through doing what is honest and integrity. It is the result of confidence and trust from other people that can lead to the best reputation for business feasible.

Ming Yu

(meiyo)

Honor

"You can abandon your own body, but never let go of your honor."

- Miyamoto Musashi

The teacher was famous who administered an Maths exam. It was a tiny one. Within the system of schools, there were two big exams per year, and the other was the national tests, that were held every couple of years. This was small tests, so which could be referred to as the equivalent of a test. The Maths instructor suddenly stood up and stated, "Do not cheat! If you don't succeed, do it without shame!" Well. All the students were amazed. In a flash, he might be in armor commanding a cavalry unit during the time of ancient Japan. Then what's honor? which you might even have even if you don't?

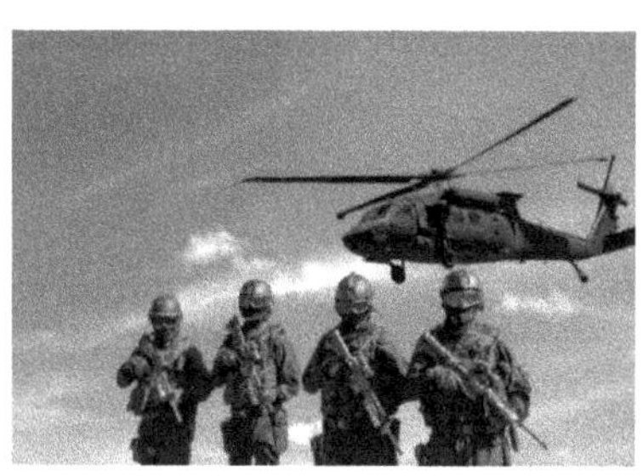

Pride is the source of honor. Self-respect is the foundation of honor. Honor is the sum of all 8 these virtues that are associated with the Samurai together. Honor is in honesty and compassion. It is also a sign of dedication. Honesty was at the heart that made the class of Samurai. Honor is a colossal thing - think of the case of cheating on an Maths test. One might argue "But it was just a small quiz, no big deal" and you could reply, "There is no big or small thing in the honor of others. Honor is all that matters".

Did you know about the Spartan phrase, used by Spartan mothers and wives to sons and husbands prior to when going to war "Come back with your shield or on it"? The purpose behind the phrase is that Spartan warriors were to return triumphant, or perhaps not ever. Consider for a moment that your mother telling the child that they should be successful (in the direction you set out to accomplish on the day) or else not.

The Japanese also have a saying similar to, "Do not return home unless you are caparisoned in brocade" This is the concept is that the Samurai will have to earn high honors and then be awarded by a position of higher rank and the ability to be dressed up in luxurious silks, brocade, and so on. It should be clear the importance of honor to each culture; living without honor wasn't living at all. It's either victory or death, as the saying goes.

The most extreme part of Samurai honour is known as "Seppuku" - a form of suicide that requires you to cut yourself in order to restore your dignity. In spite of how horrible it would be to cut the stomach of your own but what's the point? What does it have to have to do with respect?

It is how high the Samurai valued honor and the value it had and was only attainable through extremely extreme means and only after making the biggest sacrifice possible and your life. This is the only way to be restored to honor and live in a dignified manner.

If you are a Samurai says the action he will perform the action is perfect as it gets. There is no need to promise that he will do or say exactly the same.

"Reputation is the impression that other people think of your character. The way you define honor is by what you think about your self."

- Lois McMaster Bujold

Let me ask you: how many people and women at your company would you be confident as an honorable person? There are anyone? You may be aware of some decent workers, good employees, and competent workers however, let's suppose your workplace has a staff of 100 Few of the people you are aware of can be considered honorable.

That's not saying that there isn't however, since there may not have had the chance to carry out any conspicuously moral act, and there's been no burning buildings that they could rescue victims from, or villains to take on. But, is there even one? That's not at all surprising; after all, if honour were normal or simple to attain, it wouldn't be as valuable which is why this statement highlights the significance of honour. So, what do you want to be the most honorable individual at work? If the company management needs to raise someone's status or choose the person to lead a initiative, your name will surely be in the conversation!

How do you be able to show honor at work? Since I said earlier that there aren't many occasions to display honor at the peaceful workplace of a corporation. Any person working in a corporate setting reading this book is aware of how hard it can be to stand out by your work at a large corporation or even be recognized because of your personal qualities.

Just like any successful endeavor is, it requires patience, time and effort. It is essential to adhere to the core values you hold dear and uphold the rule of law and always make an ethical choice rather than choosing the best option. The concept of honor is similar to that of reputation because it must be constructed one step at a time as well as brick-by-brick. Nobody enters a room and says"I'm honourable!" To put it into a single sentence: should you be considered honorable and choose to live your honor, do so. But, of course, I'm also not suggesting that you sacrifice your life in the same way as the Samurai however, you should set this as your objective. When faced with a difficult choice make it clear that you have an option between your life or honour, and make the choice of honor.

Let's look at the world of business. Did you remember what I wrote about reliability and integrity before? Honor is better than integrity for the businessperson. Imagine it as being a gentleman with a high-quality designation.

Sir, Baron Earl, Marquis, Count and Duke. It's natural to assume that someone with a higher status like Duke naturally has greater authority, power as well as more money than the Earl, Baron or even an.

Therefore, Integrity, Reliability Honourable, and Integrity are similar names in the world of business. The Honorable Businessman ranks very much in the upper echelon of his class. This reputation and honor is built incrementally through each business transaction or payment, as well as an respected contract until the businessperson is in the top position of respect across the world.

It's in some ways superior to a noble title because it's not bought nor passed down through inheritance; it's obtained and earned which is why it's appreciated for it. It's been said before that something which cannot be purchased with money is unattainable.

There are wealthy motorists with expensive vehicles or in lavish homes, but you'll feel confident that you own something isn't theirs, despite the wealth they have. In some instances it is possible that you are higher than their wealth in HONOR.

Then it comes down to the issue of what do you do in the event that you are unable to honor your name?

It is normal to make mistakes. an error can ruin the reputation of 20 years of honest dealings. We are fortunate that we don't have be a slave to seppuku just to recover our dignity. If you commit mistakes and the whole thing your efforts are lost Do not be depressed. The only thing you can do is and start again. Begin to build respect and honor starting from scratch no matter the length of time it takes, you'll get there!

Zhong Yi

(chugi)

Loyalty

"Duty is heavy as a mountain but Death is lighter than a feather."

- GunjinChokuyu, 1882

The Samurai's obligation was to his Lord. He was loyal towards his Lord. It may seem like common sense since everyone has an obligation or a loyalty to another person. The Emperor is the only exception of this rule and yet, when you add the phrase "unto death" to that sentence and the phrase takes on an entirely new definition. The duty of a Samurai was towards his Lord until the end of time. Samurai's duty and loyalty was to his Lord unto death. Samurai willingly gave up his life in service to his Lord even if asked to sacrifice his life.

It was true that the practice did exist. There were times when a god would instruct an Samurai to perform seppuku. This Samurai will obey with aplomb to then immediately dismember his body. What type of devotion does need to show in order to accomplish this? What kind of a person must be to offer all of his life for the sake of what the request was made to him? Answer: As faithful as the Samurai.

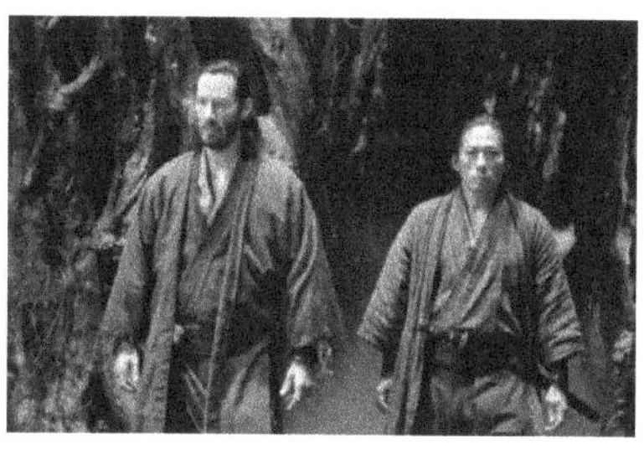

Like the Samurai. This is the meaning behind being loyalty to the end of time - the absolute loyalty and duty demands the surrender of everything that you own all the way to your entire life. What is more to offer? All you have done is give to the Lord of your life.

Let us look at the story of 47 Ronin (Masterless Samurai) (Lang Ren . Their Lord

They were swindled and forced to seppuku in the hands of an official of the highest rank in the court. In the present, the law of the Samurai demands anyone Samurai to be vengeful towards his Lord's murderer.

The Shogun (the most strong Lord in Japan) (Jiang Jun)) was a powerful Lord.

He ordered that there be no retribution taken in or by the Samurai of the Lord who had been betrayed. Additionally, rather than trusting the Samurai to follow the orders and follow the order, the chief Samurai for the Lord supervised for 1.5 years to determine whether he was willing to try anything. What was that Samurai perform? He played the role of a drunk during 1.5 years.

He was drunk and reckless during the 1.5 years during which was under surveillance until the spies pulled away, and he along with the other 46 Samurais walked to the residence of a judge and executed him.

The story doesn't end with the story, but. The 47 Ronin were rebels against the orders of the Shogun and, according to law, were considered criminals (although according to the Samurai code, they were faithful Samurai) and were to be executed. But due to the public support who voted for them, the Shogun acknowledged their loyalty to the law and permitted them to execute seppuku "honorably" (to the Samurai the Samurai, it was disgraceful to be executed for committing a crime and being sentenced to it was a fitting death to die through the sword as well as seppuku). While this isn't as spooky as it may seem, it's thought to be a happy conclusion because they were able to avenge their Lord, and they were not hanging, however they were given honorable executions.

However, my focus is on the fact that the people of 47 Ronin had a full understanding of the repercussions for disobeying the Shogun and were not expecting honorable death. However, even if they were successful however, they knew they'd be astonished at the execution which was a horrible fate for the typical Samurai but they didn't hesitate to commit the act. The story about the legendary 47 Ronin has become a symbol with Japan for loyalty and service whatever the cost.

The Samurai is accountable for his actions as well as their effects, as well as faithful to the people under his control. The loyalty of a Samurai to his Daimyo cannot be doubted.

"Respect can be earned. Honesty is rewarded. The trust is earned. The loyalty is rewarded"

- Anonymous

Obligation to your family.Duty towards your friends.Duty towards your nation. These notions are not gone at all, and they aren't even. The family has been diminished and less valuable in the age of change, friendship transforming into the notion that "every man for himself" as well as the concept of patriotism fading away since corruption and betrayals from authorities cause citizens to disbelieve in the concept of duty; it is not gone from our culture.

Naturally, it is different in the same way as it did earlier, because our beliefs and values have evolved - it's no longer the responsibility of a child to their parents to get married to whomever they have picked for them. Neither is it generally considered that you must help your country in every aspect it undertakes.

The duty to serve until death... doesn't seem to be required in the present era. It's not the case for those working in offices and businesses. Perhaps for soldiers.However commitment and loyalty are essential as well as sought-after by workers or business associates. Certain levels of loyalty is required by employers, in return for their salary... however, naturally it's not as loyal since it's purchased... but without a huge cost either.

However, we have to show loyalty to our employers and duty as it's, and are expected to fulfill these duties with a sense of. Eye for eye is a lot of loyalty. We've received our money and must be faithful in the sense to which we get paid.

It's a bit more pertinent to employees than businessmen. Businessmen have a duty of loyalties to business associates, along with their suppliers, vendors and customers. It is a bond of loyalty that is built on mutual profits as well as past contributions and gratifications. It is also to ensure to ensure the continuation of these profits as well as favors i.e. it's loyalty founded upon self-interest that is well-informed that creates a firm bonds to loyalty.

What else should be added? Keep your word, as it's beneficial for your businesses. Do you think that's enough? But I'd like to include an additional caveat to that assertion... Be loyal to people who are worth your loyalty, as it's beneficial for your the business. There. There's no need to go into detail about what can occur to you or your company if you put your trust, loyalty and confidence to a shady business partner you think?

There's nothing bad about the fact that the notion of loyalty has changed. like we said earlier it was not uncommon to find people in the past who believed loyalty was ALL and everything, so much that they sacrificed their morals to prove their loyalty. It is now a more rational day, when we recognize that the importance of righteousness must be over loyalty. The cost we have paid for this progress is unfortunately the diminishing notion of loyalty which is prevalent in the present.

Zi Zhi

(jisei)

Chapter 4: Self-Control

"Fast like the wind,"

Like a quiet forest intrusive as a fire

It is immobile as an edifice."

- Takeda Shingen

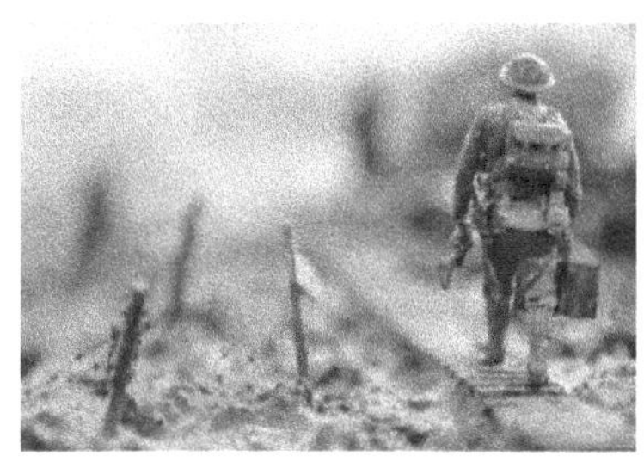

If you had to picture the person who would be a warrior. What kind of character would pop into your thoughts? A fervent and emotional fighter? Or, a cold and heartless killer? There were many combat cultures through our time that have different opinions on what is the "appropriate" personality for a warrior.

A Samurai can be described as a warrior who has an iron control system - not joyous or angry, not indifferent or cold, it will be a soldier who does not reveal his emotions to his adversaries, since He keeps himself in check.

There is a saying it is said that "Knowledge is Power", and this is especially applicable to the Samurai. If the enemy is aware of the thoughts you have, emotions or your thoughts they have control over you and has the power to degrade or even defeat you.

Control was therefore a vital characteristic that Samurai. It was a must for a Samurai to possess for him to avoid having to expose weaknesses or allow adversaries to take advantage of. The Samurai was also considered to be unacceptable to be the Samurai to express emotions through his face. It was also believed that the Samurai didn't show any affection towards family members when they were in public this could have taken things to an extreme. But that was their faith of discipline and self-control.

The ability to control oneself by the Samurai did not limit themselves only in the realm of emotions or mind The Samurai were first and foremost fighters. The control of the body was a must to the Samurai. Lust, greed, and sloth and all the other "sins of the flesh" were not allowed for the Samurai.

Physical control of limbs, muscles and muscles was required in order to be able to effectively fight in combat - the ultimate of Samurai swordfighting methods was to be "One with the sword" Absolute self-control of one's body was required to reach the ideal.

I believe that the demonstration of absolute self-control and the results you could achieve by it, are best demonstrated by this story from the warring period of

Japan however, the individual who displayed the self-control demonstrated was not an honourable Samurai and shouldn't be imitated. The name of the person was Ukifune Jinnai. He was a ninja and an Japanese assassin. He had the job of assassinating UesugiKenshin(mentioned earlier in this book), who was protected by Samurai and his OWNteam of ninjas, ANDa team of ninjas had previously tried to assassinate Kenshin and failed, so Kenshin was on full alert.

To make a long story shorter, Jinnai infiltrated Kenshin's castle and avoided the guards and then climbed inside the toilet (old fashion Japanese toilets were basically a hole with chutes leading to the bottom) and was waiting until Kenshin was ready to the bathroom and then stabbed the king by using the spear.

Then, think about the emotions Jinnai might have felt and went through the obstacles to complete this task. Jinnai was not aware the significance of this act.

Kenshin used the toilet (the castle was home to many toilets obviously) and had to stand in mid-air and prop himself against the wall of the chute, and hang the position until Kenshin arrived, with the worry of being discovered and he wouldn't be able to get out, stuck in a toilet... control over his body, his mind and his feelings, Jinnai could control them every one of them. As a result his success in the murder.

What can we take out of this story? Sure, Jinnai was a villain. An assassin. What is the reason we are studying the story of his life? It's not to praise his deeds or the success he achieved, not at all. It is important to remember that the exact principles that are based on the same principles, practices, and beliefs can be beneficial to anyone who practice them.

Self-control is do not just benefit the good and even the most vile of people recognize the benefits.

Only way for us to take on the devils that lurk in OURreality is to understand the values and practices of these people and to be more successful than they already are. Can it be done? Absolutely not. There's no way to say that becoming an Samurai was simple - it can be a rewarding experience.

"Respect comes from earning it. Honesty is valued. It is a sign of trust. The loyalty is rewarded"

- Anonymous

Self-control and discipline have disappeared from our radars of our modern world. We won't name individuals, however it is clear from the statistics that some countries have a significant portion of population is obese or overweight. It is because from the fact that self-control is which isn't being practiced or accepted in those nations anymore. I'm certain that I do not want to get into the topic of abuse of drugs and the complete lack of self-control until the person is able to commit self-destruction.

In some countries, there is a lack of self-control from their citizens that they make laws that allow for acts committed by anger, or with extreme emotions. Self-control is a characteristic isn't a priority across many different cultures, however this is nothing to do with be related to YOU exercising the art of self-control. There is no need for assistance from anyone else or any encouragement to exercise self-control. After all, it's YOURSELF that you are trying to be in control of, not the other. Self-control involves looking within.

Understanding its significance and applying this in your own lives is sufficient; however, when the general public does not believe in self-control (maybe self-restraint might be more accurate) it is impossible to aid those who do. Lust, anger Are there situations when giving into those desires can result in the best outcome?

When you are an employee who is dependent on others, self-control is vital to retain your job. It's very similar to being a Samurai in the real sense. They were subordinate to Lords and superiors and had to obey orders they might not have been able to agree with. One difference between them as employees and the ones we have in our present day is that the employee is able to resign and then seek work with a different company.

With that said I'm certain that readers who been employed before understand the stress of having changing jobs or even to go through job interview. It's not a great decision to quit your job without a reason and then walk away and then have difficulty getting a new job and then run out of cash in the interim. Therefore, self-control is essential!

If your employer has been deemed insensitive, or unkind or is in the tendency of making poor choices and then blames your actions, please avoid expressing outrage or react to their demands. Simply nod and control your anger, and submit to a new job immediately. Be sure not to allow your life or your plans get ruined by people who make you feel uncomfortable.

Being a businessman is a professional, there are numerous occasions where self-control may be necessary, either for the sake of profit or to prevent loss. If you are planning to do something that might be impacted due to interference from rivals

You must refrain from divulging any details about plans to anyone that could lead to leaks of data. If you've been deceived or lied to by your business associates or close friends, you'll be required to repress your fury as well as "admit defeat" - or just be self-controlled.

There is no perfect success rate in business. there will be occasions where you fall short or feel beat or defeated, and revealing the emotions of your enemies during that time will be a bonus point for your victory over them. Make sure to control yourself and keep your feelings hidden within your soul, and let your adversaries know that you are not in weaknesses; just wait for the chance to make it even.

However badly you've been wronged it is not a good idea sharing your ideas or feelings with your adversaries - make sure no one know, or suspect the plans you have made and your odds of achieving your goals will be significantly increased.

There's an old Japanese expression that says "Even a lone mutter in a well is known after three years". It is a clear message: any information is not kept within your soul will end up being exposed in the future. Limit your willingness to divulge your thoughts and ideas with the world and keep them in your own heart.

A Simple Choice

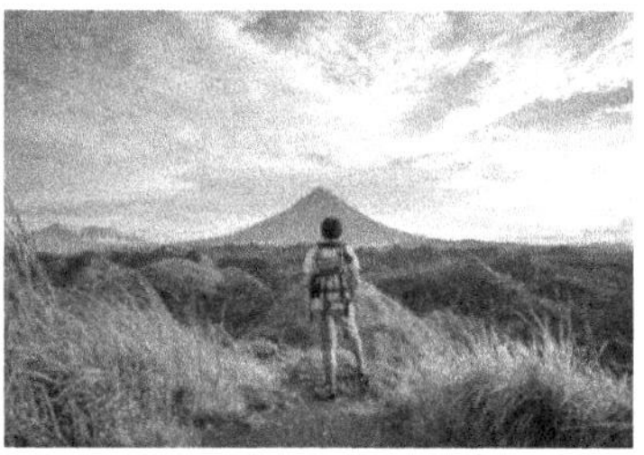

We are now at the final chapter We have a decision. A simple question. Shakespeare once wrote "To be or not to be, that is the question." It's the sole inquiry.

Are you looking to practice Bushido throughout your life? Do you wish to learn the footsteps of the old Samurai? This is the most basic question that you will need to decide is whether you want to or not?

It is not your responsibility to the author or to the mythical Samurai. Your answer lies within the person you are... Yes... either... No. You can choose to Bushido.To living a life that is virtuous. Choose your path and then live by the choice.

Bonus - 10 Samurai Principles for Guidance

These are the basic rules to guide you along your way:

TheSamurai: Becomea Master to Yourself

Make a commitment to your higher objective in the world.

Open to Suggestions, Accept Challenges &Remain Resourceful

Accept, adjust and add benefits through the use of Solutions that are flexible, adaptable and provide value.

StrikeSwiftlywith Accurate Precision

Recognize weak spots and resolve the situation swiftly.

BeFirm &Resolute

Make a position and hold your position with vigilance under all pressures.

Anticipate &Accessthe Complications & Risks

Think about the whole picture to strategize, and consider the implications.

Confront Your BattleCourageously

Never give up fighting for an issue that you firmly are a believer in.

Don't Engage in AttritionBattles

Concentrate on yourself, as arguments distract you from your goal.

Managing theExpectations of Yourself&Others

The true peace and satisfaction are only possible by being faithful to the path.

BeRespectfuland PracticeProfessional Integrity

Keep your faith in the Lord since honor has no limits.

BeSelectiveof YourCompanions and Workas a Team to Accomplish Greatness

Be an inspiration to your friends and family members, and give back your knowledge.

Chapter 5: The History of the Bushido Code Principles of Samurai Culture

The Bushido code of conduct tightly linked to Samurai ethics was instrumental in promoting Asian architectural styles, Japanese ideals, and various popular traditions like tea ceremonies, and the Samurai sword-making tradition. In the absence of a written code of gentlemanly behavior, Bushido eventually became the foundation of the Japanese ethics teaching the principles of which are relevant to this day. Here are our editors talking about the historical background of the Bushido or Samurai code of conduct, as well as contemporary interpretations of how it can extend to our daily lives.

What is Bushido?

Bushido is a code of ethics which originated with The Samurai (or Samurai soldiers of Japan that were able to spread their ideals throughout society. They were influenced by Confucianism as generally a conservative religion and beliefs system that puts the greatest importance to loyalty as well as responsibility. The Bushido Code of conduct contains eight core ideas or principles that were designed to be embraced by warriors.

The Eight Principles

Justice The concept of justice is an essential Samurai principle. Implementing the Bushido concept of justice in your daily life demands that you concentrate on the right thing and maintain the value of a morally upright quality of character.

Courage: In contrast to justice, courage requires understanding of the difference between correct and what is not. Courage requires more than just the ability to discern but also the capacity to be able to act.

Compassion: Compassion refers to the capacity of empathy to express compassion and understanding. Also, it requires the ability to look at the world through the eyes of another. This is an especially important feature for those who are who are in leadership positions.

Respect: Respect implies that you recognize the value of the experiences of others and their emotions. It is important to practice politeness when you be able to work well with others.

Integrity: In order to live by the many other declared principles, you must be committed to the principles of honesty. It's about living a life of honesty and integrity.

Honor Samurai were warriors that had a belief in their own worth and followed the most ethical code of conduct. The moral obligation is to acknowledge your obligation and honor the code of conduct.

Loyalty: Be true to your self, all the time. If it is possible to show loyalty to another person, even in stressful circumstances, it must not be rescinded.

Self-control in all circumstances when with people and on your own, self-control within the Bushido code is adhering to the Bushido Code.

Origin of the Bushido Code

The term 'bushido an acronym for the military that is also the source of the phrase 'bushido.' The term'samurai' is roughly translated as 'people who are serving,' however it has evolved to mean an individual who fights. To comprehend the underlying principles to this Bushido code, it's necessary examine the background of the Samurai.

The history of the Samurai started around the time of the 8th century, when horses were used as the ally of landowners with wealth. are referred to as Samurai. In the 12th century, the control of land was changed within Japan and the dictatorship of the military called the Kamakura Shogunate came into being. In this time, Samurai usage was popularized by the political elite and their superior position was formally established.

In the aftermath of a turbulent time that culminated with the Mongol invasion threatening the stability of the administration, which led to the conclusion of Kamakura period at the close in the 14th century the Tokugawa Shogunate was a long period of peace. The Samurai weren't needed to be a source of military power in the time of peace and prosperity, rather, they were asked to be the head of the state. Gradually they were elevated from a role of a knight into embracing all the duties of an official from government.

The Japanese styles of art that were common to the Samurai developed in the Tokugawa time period. This included tea ceremonies, flowers, gardens in the rock as well as a distinct design of Japanese art created in the Edo period.

The Military Houses Ordinance, or the Buke shohatto, was issued in 1615. During this time, the Samurai were required to not just to be taught in authority, but also how to conduct themselves in manners of conduct and civility. This was the time when the Bushido principles were developed as the codes of conduct that were adopted by the Japanese populace all over the world, greatly influenced by Samurai, Buddhism, and Confucianism and Confucianism. The Samurai concept was established as the ideal of a man who was refined.

Bushido code is a way to express gratitude. Bushido code, as a general level, demands reverence and respect for all living things, and suggests to be exemplary, show kindness, and be kind to others.

Modern Bushido

Japan has also established a conscripted army following the ruling samurai class deposed in the aftermath of Meiji Restoration. There is a chance that bushido as well as the samurai that developed it would go away.

But, through the beginning of the 20th century as well as World War II, Japanese dictators and fascists continued to abide by this traditional ideal. Seppuku-like parallels could be seen in the admonitions to assassination Japanese soldiers had made against a variety of Pacific Islands, as well as the kamikaze pilots who rammed their planes into Allied battleships, and then bombed Hawaii in order to initiate American participation in World War II.

In modern Japanese traditions, bushido is still used to be practiced even today. The emphasis he places on confidence as well as self-denial can be particularly helpful in companies that are attempting to figure out the details of their "salarymen" to get the maximum amount of work done.

Bushido: The Samurai Code Of Honor

The Samurai weren't the mercenary guerrillas that were roaming about Japan and fighting for the amount of money a warlords would offer them. They were obligated by law and honor to a certain daimyo or lord and committed to duty and honor to their local community.

The code of honor called Bushido and is the result of the word bushi which is a reference to "warrior." It is a Japanese word actually means "the way." This is why Bushido refers to "the path of the warrior." This is a code that originated in the past, when Samurai were horsemen and archers. The dedication and discipline required to study these methods and to bond with horses has led to Kyuba and no Michi, "the horse and bow style." Even though Bushido is often referred to as code, every Samurai did not follow a specific rulebook. Indeed, through Japanese the history of Japan, Bushido changed significantly, and sometimes even between clans to another. Bushido wasn't documented until the 17th century even after decades of samurai-style life.

Samurai's primary duty was to be loyal to his father. Japan was a country with a feudal system that required obedience from his vassals which, in turn had the Lord's military and economic security. If a lord was not capable of relying on the absolute loyalty from his vassals the entire scheme could fail. The Japanese that would fight to the bitter end in an endless battle for the protection of their master's castle, or take their own life when they believed they had been disgraced by their Lords, usually had this feeling of honor and loyalty in extremes.

Therefore, Samurai had responsibility for the retribution. In the event that his master's reputation was damaged or his master's death occur Samurai were required to find the culprits and kill their enemies.

Chapter 6: A Code of Conduct

The Samurai languages used in movies might not be the same one that you experienced when watching films. However, if you spend the time to watch or read the text, you'll find that a lot of the principal characters ' motivations, as well as the primary motivation behind the story's unfolding and unfolding, have been influenced by the centuries-old codes and practices. Though some may feel this is an oversimplification but it's an educational issue and should not be considered a full analysis of films about martial arts. However, when you go at the past and think about what martial arts have taught us today, and what principles students learn alongside self-defense and self-defense, this is a crucial factor to take into consideration. The most straightforward way to think about the code of conduct from the perspective of contemporary culture and some historical context as well as the world of pop culture.

This is where you'll discover impressive information on the topic, which is in Nitobe's "Bushido: The Soul of Japan." It explained the way in which actions were taken that the Samurai's order of samurai performed and also the code of ethics that chivalry must be displayed. It is evident that it is happening, and that we're beginning to witness an exciting branching route that has eight virtues which are entrusted to aristocracy. This book reveals certain ideas that were showcased in films and brings back a not-living-class system.

Understanding the Bigger Picture

For those who study, it could be a bit far-fetched to look at the concept the idea that Hong Kong action cinema and the notion that there are eight virtues in the Samurai code of conduct are in some way similar. It's important to realize that presentation of this topic is not intended to be a lecture. This is intended to highlight that you must show the reverence of the present martial arts practitioner, as well as the principles that were established over time. If you're learning the art of karate, aikido or kung fu, ninjitsu or another form of martial art, some techniques date back to centuries and it is important to be devoted to all virtues. Like religious believers who rely the tenets of their faith founded upon their faith in the Holy Book, martial artists adhere to the principles which are incorporated in the tradition of self-defense. To better understand the idea of the both the past and the present an analysis of the fundamentals in Samurai Code Samurai Code is in order.

Bushido is the right name used to refer to"the" Code of Samurai. It means "The

Warrior's Way." The Bushido enforced restrictions on Samurai which prevented their doing specific things as well as living a normal lifestyle. This is not only beneficial for Samurai however, it's ideal for everybody because it makes everyone that follows it a better person.

Ways Of The Samurai: The Bushido Code And Its Virtues

The commitment and effort necessary to develop the skills of a Samurai were incredibly impressive. They required a solid bond with their horses and eventually Kyuba No Michi or "Horse's Way & Bow."

While it's called a manual, it's not a collection of rules which every Samurai follow. The codes have changed over the course of the development of the country, ranging from an influential clan to the following. It was not released in the end of

17th century. The text was published after years of living the lives of the Samurai Warriors.

Below is a listing of the fundamentals of the Samurai's Bushido code.

Gi - Rectitude or Justice

Resilience or Justice, Gi is the highest virtue of the code. Gi's simpler definition stems from an infamous background samurai. Gi claims that the definition of rightness is the capacity to select the right path to take without hesitation. It's done without any hesitation or second thoughts.

A second well-known fighter is a different opinion on the Bushido. The pillar of justice is a symbol of respect and solidity. It is impossible for the head to rest on the top of the spine without bones. The hands aren't mobile, and feet can't be able to walk. Also, with out Gi or learning, neither aptitude can help one become an excellent Samurai.

Yu - Courage

It is essential to know what's correct and what is not. The person who is courageous must understand and then act according to. The Bushido is able to distinguish between bravery and grit. Courage is one of the virtues that can be expressed through the righteousness and prudence.

Confucius defines bravery in his collection. Confucius says that "perceiving as well and acting in the way that is appropriate doesn't demonstrate the absence of bravery. That's what is the truth.

Jin - Compassion

Jin is the love which connects us all. Showing compassion and love with perseverance is the art. Jin is also required to see the world through an other's perspective; this is an essential trait to every leader around him.

The Samurai are able to kill soldiers, however, benevolence keeps them firmly in their thought processes. The key is to get compassion and grace in the appropriate moment. The Samurai should know they're doing only the right cause.

It was done for good reason and for conviction, if it was necessary to murder someone. Furthermore it is believed that the Samurai ensure that they don't need to strike and will demonstrate mercy and compassion.

Rie - Respect

They are generally also polite towards their adversaries. They have a morally upright mindset that does not require them to show their power. In this way, the true strength of a rebel is only revealed in difficult situations.

It's not easy to discern the distinction between reverence and politeness. In Bushido respect for others, it is the foundation by a genuine man generosity and appreciation. It is an act in a manner that is respectful of other people's sentiments. It's not a good character trait if just being afraid of offending someone's nice person would push the person to do it.

Makoto - Integrity

In order to practice the other Bushido principles, Makoto or Honor should be maintained. It means that you should live honestly and honestly. It is an act of cowardice and is a disgrace to the honorable. People's words ought to be the result of truthfulness and honesty. of integrity and honesty will be his approach towards be a warrior.

The Code declares that abstinence and simplicity are a part of being honest. The wealthy can hinder knowing, while the need for thriftiness can increase the level of honesty. There is an honest and transparent approach to everything you say and do. The title of Samurai warriors is their seal. Samurai warrior acts as their signature that never fails to be a part of their identity.

Meiyo - Honor

Professional Samurai who held self-esteem, adhered to the most ethical guidelines for ethics. To promote the virtues of honor, their moral duties should be recollected.

While the Bushido concentrates on combat, non-martial behaviour remains a part of. The sense of honor he displayed is what differentiates the distinction of a Samurai. This is an intense awareness of the importance and dignity of one's own life. Additionally the fact that it is also a sign that a Samurai was taught in the role of a warrior, and he was expected to honor his rights and obligations.

The fear and worry about being disgraced can be a source of frustration for everyone Samurai warrior's brain. However, these warriors have certain attitudes due to their culture. They aren't irritated by any slightest annoyance. It is done to avoid any all criticism and are known to be quick-tempered.

"Real endurance only means being able to endure the intolerable," according to a well-known quote says.

Chuugi - Loyalty

The concept of loyalty is one of the main components of the Bushido. The Samurai were considered to be close friends. They therefore did whatever they could to defend and aid their fellow soldiers.

It was important to be loyal because it signified that the Samurai had the confidence of everyone else. In addition, they believed that the guerrillas were loyal to everything they undertake. There's no reason to worry about losing the battle, neither.

Jisei - Character & Self-Control

The Bushido suggests that one must follow a timeless moral code. The other one is over the line of logic. The thing that is wrong will be incorrect, while what's true will be correct. It is possible to distinguish between right and wrong as well as wrong, right, and. They aren't things which can be debated or debate, but one needs to be aware of the distinction between them.

It is the duty that of Samurai warriors Samurai warrior to educate his young ones about morality. The way to do this is evident in the actions he takes.

The education of the warrior was focused on establishing a kind of personality. Implicit intelligence as well as prudence and the ability to speak dialectically weren't important. There was a superiority in intellect attained by these warriors. However, the typical Samurai was generally a warrior of the fight.

The Secret Power Of Discipline

Do you know the link to your career or job with your thoughts and the results you're enjoying and do you not? If you can learn to regulate your thoughts towards an optimistic mindset are you confident that you'll succeed?

Self-disciplinary approach. We'll be real. This is a process in progress for the majority of us. covered in a veneer of positive intentions, fear, and a sense of defeat. It's just not what it's supposed to be. Just like everything else, self-control is an exercise. It's not going to be perfect each day, but each day -- with its failures and successescan be a step forward, and it's all about discipline.

I've completed the steps needed for building self-discipline which you can implement today. This chapter and an understanding of self-control is, will give you the skills that you require to develop self-discipline learning in all you do.

Chapter 7: What is Self-Discipline?

A desire to accomplish exactly what you're supposed to do requires self-discipline. Certain self-discipline involves putting aside the instant gratification, or goals for longer-term achievement. If, for instance, you are looking to get well-maintained, then you will be able to tolerate 5 a.m. a.m. temporary pain. Training days are a great way to reap longer-term advantages of being fit and feeling great.

Doctor. Steve Peters states in "The Chimp Illusion" that our minds are already what that we would like to be. The mind's subconscious keeps our minds from thinking in the way we're required to get the optimal scenario. Discipline and self-control allow us to take the physical force and defeat our anxiety-ridden mind.

The process of developing self-discipline goes beyond simply helping you move forward through your day. The benefits of helping others have been demonstrated:

Attain Long-Term Goals For those who want to achieve more impactful goal-setting, longer-term objectives, self-discipline lets people ward off the urges to be in a hurry. Through her research in 2016 about perseverance and "passion for long-term goals," commonly referred to as grit Grit expert Angela Duckworth speaks to this. The study she conducted revealed it was that "attaining challenging goals involves not only talent but also a sustained and focused application of talent over time," also known as self-control.

Reduce Anxiety - All of us are guilty of being stressed. It's common for people to be confused when they feel bad emotion by talking or doing something about other things. Indeed, a study conducted in 2016 showed that increasing self-control on examinations can aid students deal with anxiety-related problems.

Improve Physical Health - This seems obvious enough and yet those with consistent self-control are more likely to avoid the consumption of alcohol and tobacco alcohol that can harm overall health. Controlling oneself can also lead to reduced rates of obesity and dependency.

Positively impact relationships - Yes you can be enhanced by self-control. Psychology claims that "The capacity to self-control is an ability to take empathetic perspective-- the ability to move beyond one's point of view." When we take these steps that we can overpower our defense reactions and cultivate more positive attitude that can lead to more positive and more enduring relationships.

Develop a greater resilience - In the event of an event of adversity, are you able to recover quickly? The ability to discipline yourself can be a indicator. The stronger you're at it, the more power you will have to resist urges and delay satisfaction. Psychology Today says, "A positive person believes in their ability to effectively handle the problems and circumstances of life."

Feel More Happy - The more inventive and content you feel your productivity will increase. can be. As we become more confident in our charge of the behavior that is causing us to be and the more feelings of happiness we experiencewhich in turn can make us happier!

How To Build Self Discipline?

Know Where You Struggle

Write down everything you're doing during the day. Next, discuss your beliefs and then ask yourself whether your convictions are expressed by the actions you take. You probably have a handful of activities you engage in each day that do not reflect these values (hey it's human- We are all human and have some).

It can be helpful to solicit for comments from coworkers parents, teachers, or even family members that know us well in the initial phase of identification. Check for overlaps with how others view your conduct and what shortcomings have been spotted by you.

After you've made progress in some aspects, you can put together an action plan such as "One one of my flaws is the tendency to put off making calls until late in the morning. In the course of the week it slows me down and can make it challenging to get there. I'm planning to conduct X calls on my first day tomorrow after I'm at the office.

Know How You Succeed

Begin by welcoming your colleagues. inquire about the evenings they spend with them. An afternoon coffee to the kitchen. Lunch and a chat with the team. A local coffee shop for or a stroll in the afternoon. Each of these small excursions adds into a lot of free time. Making connections with colleagues is essential, as is taking physical and mental breaks during the entire day.

Being honest about how you work is equally important. If you find your mornings consumed with events not connected to your work, and this is the time when you're most productive -- that's not a good thing. Be aware of the time and place you're performing the best job you can.

If you're awake at 9:15 a.m. then you're set for the afternoon. Coffee breaks will be scheduled for 12 noon. Be sure to protect your ability to succeed at work. Your company will promote better health and have healthier outcomes for your company.

Identify And Write Down Clear Goals

Do you realize that when you list the goals you want to achieve, you're 41 percent more likely reach your goals? By writing down goals lets one visualize the end goal as well as the steps to achieve it and what steps one should do to achieve it.

So, set your objectives and record them in writing before you begin your journey to becoming the very best version of yourselfin your the workplace or in your private life.

Visualize Your Outcome

Memory doesn't differentiate between real experiences or thought-of. Once you have a clear picture of it with a lot of intensity, your neurochemistry of your brain changes like you were witnessing the event.

Positive results like, "If I make it to the top of our event chart, I'll treat myself to an outstanding meal," gives you satisfaction that comes with climbing up the top of the Leaderboard and reducing anxiety. It makes it much easier for you to get over the obstacles that stand in your way and to take concrete steps towards achieving your objectives.

Don't Wait For It To Feel Right

If you're waiting around for your calendar to fill up or your office clean and your mailbox at a level that is manageable your work to complete may never get started. The moment you accept the idea of possessing everything you require to perform your job at its bestdue to the fact that you do.

Start Small

Are you inspired by this selection? Are you prepared to change your old habits to become an ideal employee or dealer? Make the first step as simple as it is. After a week, changing your routine is a burning out and a disaster recipe.

Choose a couple of little habits each week that you can concentrate on. It is possible to take your cup of coffee to work in the beginning of your week, so that you don't fall into the spiral that is known as "the break room" to begin your work.

If you have a week of good luck to your credit, each Friday, after work, you'll be able to schedule a couple of hours in your schedule for administrative work including adding prospect notes to your CRM or replying to outstanding email messages. You might be surprised by how productive and organized you've gained after a few weeks of adjusting one behavior one at a time.

Get a Mentor

There are a few issues you should discuss with your coach about issues who a manager or supervisor may not feel comfortable discussing. If I'm looking to end being a slacker when I'm supposed to be pursuing leads through social media platforms and feel more comfortable, it would be better to discuss the issue with my coach, not my boss.

In general, advisors possess the most experience, understand your needs better and offer you the tips and suggestions you require to be successful, not just at your present position, but also for your future.

Practice, Fail, Start Over

The truth is that disciplined individuals do not have the time to finish all of the doughnuts that are baked in the oven, spend time on the internet for 45 minutes and then miss two chances by 10 a.m.

These are the things they do at night, and the next day they awake and are trying to make better decisions.

It is the act of trying to overcome, battling, and then trying to do it again, is self-control.

Chapter 8: Know How you'll Measure Progress

If you're not clear on the best way to measure the progress, it will be difficult to know whether you're succeeding. If the goal for you in the first part of this month is to set up more meetings, begin with determining the number of meetings you'd like to set up. Work backwards and figure out how many meetings per week will be required as well as the time each one is expected to take.

Determine what success means after you've established the exact goals of your project. Will you aim to get the number you want? What happens in the event that a meeting scheduled for last-minute fails to be held? Does the event need to be a demonstration? Decide what you want to be successful, so that you know how to measure the outcome.

Take Care Of Yourself

If you can't bear in this way, your discipline will be of no value. We all work in the occasional 28-hour workday (those exist, don't they?) But If you've been burning the midnight oil for a few weeks or even months, and then end up becoming much more "self-disciplined," you missed the purpose.

A key part of self-discipline is taking care of yourself. Breaks throughout the day, a nutritious eating plan, enough sleeping, and balanced connections make the worldas well as usturn around. In fact, research shows that taking care practices like going for an easy walk, paying attention to five items around you or even detecting two smells, can improve productivity at work.

How To Look After Your Mental Health Using Exercise

It's a given that it's beneficial for your body to work out. But did you realize that anxiety, depression stress, and many more are important to deal with?

What Is Physical Activity?

Physical activity on a fundamental level is any exercise that requires your muscles and expends energy. One of the most appealing aspects with physical exercise is the infinite possibilities and nearly everyone will be able to find an activity to suit their needs!

It is advised to take between 75-150 minutes of activity a each week for adults of average age. This could be a moderate-intensity activities like climbing, biking, or even cycling. Or, harder exercises like swimming fast, jumping as well as aerobics or skipping using rope. Anything that raises your heart rate will make you breath faster and it feel warmer over your exercise!

Separating them into four distinct types is a great approach to examine different kinds of physical activities.

Daily Physical Activity

Adults who exercise may be a therapeutic or leisure physical activities, such as mobility (e.g. walking, walking or biking) and occupational pursuits (e.g. working) chores in the household or play and athletics or regular family or social gatherings.

Everything from commuting to the bus station, carrying bags around and climbing up stairs are all counted and add to an average adult's 150 minutes of physical activity per week.

Exercise

A purposeful exercise to increase fitness or overall health for example, jogging or cycling. You can also increase your fitness through using weights.

Play

An unstructured, spontaneous activity done in order to enjoy or have fun.

Sport

Organized and competitive sports ranging from squash and soccer to cricket. You can take part either on our own or in a group. It's a great and engaging exercise that isn't a necessity to be working out.

They can differ in their intensity, and could be high-intensity like tennis and athletics, swimming and workout classes, or low-intensity activities and sports like darts or snooker. It could be an incentive to maintain your commitment instead of focusing on something you are required to complete.

What Are The Mental Health Benefits Of Exercise?

It's not only concerned with the strength of muscles or the capacity to exercise. Training will, naturally improve your personal and physical fitness, alter your weight, enhance sexual health, as well as add years to your lifespan. However, that's not the reason behind many individuals to stay physically active.

People who exercise regularly choose to workout due to the immense sense of wellbeing. Through the daytime, they're more energetic, are more sleepy when they go to bed, have clearer memories and are at peace with themselves and their lives. For many of the common problems with mental health It's also a powerful treatment.

Regular exercise has the potential to influence anxiety, depression, ADHD, and more significantly. Stress is relieved, increases concentration, enables people to rest better, and boosts your mood generally. To reap the benefits it's not necessary to be an exercise enthusiast. Studies suggest that even a small amount of exercise could help. It is possible to learn how to utilize exercising as a tool to improve your health, regardless of age, or level of fitness.

Exercise and Depression

Research suggests that meditation can help with depression, as does antidepressants, and, of course with no negative side consequences. Recent research conducted of The Harvard T.H. Chang School of Public Health In one instance, the Harvard T.H. Chang School of Public Health found that getting active for 15 minutes per day, or for one hour lowers the likelihood of serious depression by 26 percent. Studies also show that aside from relieving the symptoms of depression, sticking to regular exercise regimens will stop your from recurring.

Meditation has many benefits. It is a highly effective treatment for anxiety. In particular, it helps facilitate the brain to undergo a variety of modifications, such as neuronal growth reduced stress and different patterns of behaviour that promote calm and good emotional states. Also, it produces endorphins, powerful hormones that boost your brain and help you feel relaxed in your brain. At some point, meditation may provide a way to relax and allow you to take an hour of peace to get away from anxious thoughts.

Exercise and Anxiety

Exercise is an established anti-anxiety treatment that is secure and efficient. It eases tension and stress it increases your physical and mental vitality, and boosts wellbeing because it releases endorphins. Any activity that stimulates you to exercise will benefit to reduce stress, however, if you pay more attention rather than ignoring to your phone, you'll reap a greater reward.

Be aware of such things as the sensation of your feet contacting the ground, your breathing rhythm as well as your skin's sensation of the breeze. In incorporating this dimension of awareness--reflecting on your body and how it responds when you exercise -- you will not only strengthen your physical condition more easily, but you may also be able to interrupt the stream of daily concerns that go through your mind.

Exercise and Stress

Have you noticed how you feel in a stressful situation? In particular, in your eyes your arms and chest, your muscles might be tight and causing neck or back pain, or frequent headaches. It is possible to feel tightness in your chest or a pulse that is pounding or muscle cramps. Troubles with sleep or heartburn, stomach pain, diarrhoea, and frequent urination could also manifest. In addition, the worry and stress of the physical signs will contribute to more stress and create a vicious circle between body and mind.

Training can be a successful method to stop the cycle. Exercise and the release of endorphins within the brain aids in relaxing the muscles as well as ease tension within the body. Since the mind and body are in such close contact that the mind also experience better when the body is feeling better.

Exercise and ADHD

Regular exercise is among the easiest and most efficient methods to reduce ADHD symptoms as well as improve the ability to focus attention, motivation, memory and mood. The physical activity boosts the levels of norepinephrine, dopamine and serotonin within the brain in a short time, each of these affects concentration and focus. Training can help in conjunction with ADHD medication such as Ritalin as well as Adderall in this way.

Exercise, PTSD and Trauma

There is evidence to suggest that you can assist your nervous system to "unstuck" and start moving free of the immobilization response that is characteristic of PTSD or trauma by keeping your attention on your body's sensations and the way it feels when you work out. Instead of allowing your brain to wander off, pay careful focus on your joints and muscle sensations even your inner body when the body is moving. Activities that require cross-motion and involve both legs and armssuch as walking (especially in the sand) or running and swimming, strength training and dancing are among the best alternatives.

Additionally, it has been proven that activities in the outdoors, such as the sailing, hiking mountain biking, mountain climbing, whitewater river rafting as well as skis (downhill as well as cross-country) can reduce effects of PTSD.

Chapter 9: Easy Ways to Move More That Don't Involve the Gym

Do you find yourself with less time to devote to cycling or yoga? Don't worry. Consider physical exercise as an integral part of your life, not only executing a specific job. Examine your schedule and think about ways to get yourself into the action now, then and everywhere. Do you have suggestions? We've got you covered.

Within and around your home. Cleaning the house, washing your car, cut your lawn using an electric mower, and clean the patio or pavement by using the Broom.

In the office or out and about. Take a bike or walk to an appointment rather than taking the car, eliminate elevators, learn about all possible stairs, walk quickly to the bus stop, take off 1 stop earlier and park in the rear of the parking lot, go to the store or office. You can also take an easy walk on the coffee break.

As a family. In the time of training, race through the soccer fields and make a local cycling trip as part of your schedule for the weekend and play around the backyard with your family or go canoeing at a park, take your dog for a walk to a new location

For enjoyment. Choose fruit from the orchard listen to some music or visit the beach, unwind in front of the TV, form an office bowling group or take a martial art class, dance or do yoga.

Make Exercise A Fun Part Of Your Everyday Life

It's not necessary to invest long hours at the gym or make yourself do boring, long-lasting workouts in order for the benefit from training.

Neuro-Linguistic Programming

NLP is the science of the way that individuals integrate their thoughts, emotions words, actions, and language to create their desired outcomes. The creators of NLP, John Grinder & Richard Bandler have an insatiable need to find and reproduce the structure and behavior patterns of top performers and then to help others achieve the same results, thereby reducing the time required for developing expertise as well as learning. The process of doing this is called simulation, and it is the basis of NLP. Their research was dubbed Neuro-Linguistic Programming. It examines the process of how our nervous system (neuro) transforms information received through the five senses to abstract concepts (linguistic) as well as subconscious actions (programming).

What is NLP?

NLP is a form of programming that uses neurolinguistics. (NLP) examines the internal functioning of our minds as we consider the way we think and form our goals, interests, issues, as well as how we influence, share, and make sense of our lives. NLP provides specific abilities and methods to help you make positive change, to make fresh ways of thinking, become more cooperative with people around you, and break away of old patterns, destructive behaviors, and attitudes and be more clear about what we would like to accomplish and how you can accomplish it.

NLP is the science of subjective perception developmentwhich is the connection between expression, consciousness thoughts, behavior, and patterns. It's a study of interpersonal knowledge and relationships and also the in the intrapersonal realm.

NLP is a fairly new phenomenon, which began with the University of Santa Cruz in the late 1970s, when a small group of highly skilled individuals (that is the Richard like John Bandler and John Grinder) came together to share their knowledge and experiences via disciplines. Alongside other areas that it integrates perspectives from the fields of clinical and Gestalt psychotherapy as well as family therapy, hypnotherapy as well as linguistics, data theory and the field of anthropology.

As opposed to other programs for psychotherapeutic thought that rely on the way things happen, NLP started studying individuals that are extremely adept in their field and then figuring out the ways they're doing it to ensure that, by doing similar methods, anybody can attain similar results. It aims to move beyond changes that are remedial (fixing particular problems) towards "generative" change that empowers individuals to be more effective throughout your the world.

NLP is a term that refers to the neurolinguistic program. (NLP) is a modern field of study that has only been around for a few years, dating from the mid-70s. An established body of research can be found behind NLP. NLP began as a result of the coordination of two co-founders, Richard Bandler and John Grinder, who have distinct disciplines.

At one time, Professor. Grinder worked as a instructor of linguistics at Santa Cruz University of California. Bandler was there to study computing and maths at the age of an undergraduate. However it was the Dr. Grinder had already written numerous books in the subject of linguistics, which is called Transformative Grammar.

Bandler discovered that he possessed naturally gifted in pattern-modeling and listening. He found the fact that Gestalt Therapy (a type of psychotherapy) was able to recognize and reproduce patterns with minimal exposure. He was appointed editor of Gestalt Therapy for a variety of books written by Fritz Perls. Bandler was becoming acquainted with his work with Perls started to research the techniques of Perl. He began to experiment with acquaintances using Perl's methods once Bandler realized that he could reproduce Perls methods of therapy.

Richard realized after experiencing rapid and immediate effects of the simulation, that he was able to be a model for the behavior of others. Thanks to Grinder's guidance, Bandler got an opportunity to model Virginia Satir, the world's top therapy for families. Richard could describe what he called the "seven trends" used by Virginia. After John as well as John began to apply these methods and techniques, they discovered that they could re-use their techniques in the same way to achieve the same outcomes.

A computer programmers, Richard knew that to program the world's simplest "mind" (a computer with switched on and off) it is necessary to break down the system's behavior into components and then provide the system with transparent and unambiguous messages.

John used his vast understanding of transformative grammar to this simple case. The concepts of surface and deep structure suggest that knowledge and meaning change in the human brain stem from transformative grammar. Then, they began formulating a concept about how humans can be "programmed," so to think of it.

The world-renowned Anthropologist Gregory Bateson presented Bandler and Grinder to Milton Erickson, MD. Erickson developed the coping method known as "Ericksonian Hypnosis." Hypnosis is recognized in The American Medical

Association since 1958 as an effective therapeutic technique in the course of surgical procedures. It was found that we can achieve the same results Bandler and Grinder models Erickson. A lot of NLP approaches today draw from Ericksonian models.

Bandler and Grinder developed their initial idea based on these observations, and their research of the common forces and beliefs. It was developed as an understanding of communication that gave an understanding of the way that the different languages (sensory-based and language-based) "program" us to create regular and consistent behaviours, behaviors and psychosomatic reactions. The model went beyond. It also outlined methods that use subjectivity elements for psychological improvement.

Chapter 10: History of Japanese Samurai

Samurai were first introduced into Japanese history around 1200 years back. In the past, Samurai were guardians employed by landowners of huge size or nobles. But, when the nobles and landowners began relying on Samurai to defend their property, Samurai started gaining power over their authority.

A number of groups of Samurai began to take over the areas of their employers by the force of their arms. After they had taken over this land, they began invaded the land of nobles and landowners. They constantly increased their armoury so that they would not just invading other areas, but also defend their own land from the other Samurai group.

In the meantime, Samurai noticed that their social standing was not adequate for them to be new landowners. They tried to raise their status by maintaining close relationships with the people from the imperial family, as well as with strong nobles of the government of centralization. They developed such strong relationships through offering their strength of weapons to defend and increase their property. In the end, having the power of Samurai warriors boosted their negotiation ability.

In the time that Samurai gained enough power to be a part of the federal government and began to seek top positions within the federal government. In these times and eras, the Heishi family was the most influential Samurai family. The Heishi family gave their property to Emperor Shirakawa in order to serve him.

He created He made the Heishi Family one of the strongest and strong Samurai Family.

The Heishi family was able to enjoy an influential political position and a leadership position during the time of Shirakawa but the Heishi family did not hold the position of head of the government at that time. They were believed to be "guardians" of the Emperor Shirakawa. In the event that they lost at the Battle of Dan-no-Ura against the Genji family in 1185 the emperor Goshirakawa who Heishi served had lost political power in addition. It was Goshirakawa handed the head of Genji family Yoritomo Minamoto, power to rule Japan in order that Yoritomo was able to establish the first Samurai system in Kamakura 1192 (the Kamakura Shogunate).

The Heishi Family was defeated. The Minamoto Family assumed the reigns.

The very first Shogun from Kamakura Shogunate. Kamakura Shogunate.

The Kamakura Shogun first began to assign various areas in Japan in Japan to Samurai family members, he also assigned greater and more superior parts to Genji family members and the affiliates members of the family. The purpose was to increase the group spirit among Genji family members and the families of their associates. The Shogun provided official evidence of ownership of the land for Samurai families. In return, he would grant the families new land in exchange for awards.

Naturally, the Shogun had hoped for Samurai families to show their appreciation in return. The appreciation was expressed through an unwavering loyalties towards the Shogun. Shoguns who were loyal to the Samurai families that had such strong loyalty were referred to Gokenin. Gokenin. Gokenin was the relationship between Shogun and the

Gokenin family was known as "Go-on to Ho-ko" which was a reference to a reward given by Shogun for service to the Shogun and devotion for the Shogun.

Rewards and services were the primary tenets. But, there wasn't an idea of unconditional loyalty towards the Shogun at the time. Gokenin kept their commitment to the Shogun only when they expected benefits from the Shogun in exchange for their service. Bushido is very similar to the business contract in the present. The reason for this was because Gokenin were extremely independent and confident of their army's strength. A second reason was that they were always eager to increase their territory. So, if they did not anticipate to receive new land from the Shogun then there was no need for them to remain loyal towards the Shogun.

As Gokenin anticipated the reward, they were loyal soldiers with no fear of dying. Because Gokenin believed that the Kamakura Shogun could seize more territory in battles he won in battle, the Gokenins participated and did their best to show their loyalty in the eyes of Kamakura Shogun. It was crucial since the how much they received (land) was contingent on the amount Gokenin was able to contribute to victory.

In accordance with the principles of rewards and services In accordance with the principle of reward and service, the Kamakura Shogun needed to provide reward to sustain the service of Gokenin. The Shogun was able to satisfy this principle in the event that he was able to obtain new land and offer Gokenin as a reward. When he needed to defend against Mongolian army forces between 1274-1281 (Mongol Invasion of Japan) This concept of service and reward could no longer be fulfilled. The reason for this was that there was no additional area to conquer in order to defend his your own nation against Mongol invading forces. The Kamakura Shogun was unable to grant the new territory to Gokenin who took part in combats to defend.

Gokenin left the Kamakura Shogun, who did not adhere to the principles of honor and duty no longer. It was only natural that certain Gokenin, with their massive army to be the new Shoguns in order to extend their territory. They began fighting and eventually became the head of huge or medium sized clans. Within the Gokenin families, particularly the ashikaga and Nitta families were the head of the two biggest clans. The Kamakura period ended, and the country moved to a time of civil conflict.

In the time of civil war Samurai began to think about their own deaths as well as the aftermath of death. They had to deal with their own deaths during the time. They were required to address various issues like "What is death?", "What is our life?", "How can we be salvaged as warriors." Also "Is there any way not to create karma in battles?". The time was when Samurai attempted to address the questions using Buddhist teachings. The reason for this was that Samurai as well as other people from Japan believed they were during the time of Buddhism and pessimism.

At the time of skepticism, Buddha's teachings were not heeded. Thus, Japanese believed that our world was heading towards conclusion. It was quite normal for some Japanese like Samurai who lived in an unstable and dangerous times during the civil war, to be influenced by the optimism.

Samurai that sought path to salvation began studying the Buddha's teachings including The Four Noble Truths and The Noble Eightfold Path. The goals of the Samurai were to save themselves in the event of death, to eliminate Karmas when fighting, and to always be prepared for death. In integrating Buddha's teachings along with their own personal experiences, Samurai developed Bushido as the foundation of their lives.

Chapter 11: Bushido in the Era of Civil War of Japan

Ch2-1: Bushido in the Era of Civil War of Japan

Samurai were fearful of the impact of karma's influence on the destiny for Samurai warriors. The life of Samurai was a series of fighting, and there appeared there was no method to get rid of karma in their lives. They believed they'd go to hell rather than the eternal Nirvana after their death. This was an enormous task to Samurai to get rid of karma in order that they could be part of the eternal nirvana, without affecting their fate as warriors.

According to Buddha it is necessary to achieve selflessness with doing the Right Method to reach the nirvana conditional prior to death, in order to attain the unconditional Nirvana after death. In order to be self-less, one needs to improve the equilibrium of the three subject that are mind, body and awareness by following an appropriate practice in every day life. So, Samurai hoped that they could get rid of karma when they maintained an attitude of self-denial in everyday life as well as on battlefields, by sustaining their Right Practice everyday.

The family was a famous Samurai family. After he received his ordination as a Buddhist monk and returned to the Samurai's lifestyle to support his family. But, he quit his family and became an Buddhist monk once more. He began teaching about the value of self-less living and the relation between karma and desire. The advice he offered, "Get rid of everything to have nothing," was deemed as the most effective method to attain the state of selflessness. The Buddhism doctrine was founded upon the idea of emptiness and self-reliance.

In the following years, Samurai started developing a plan for their lives in order to achieve selflessness, and consequently, the conditional nirvana. They believed they could keep their self-control even in the most brutal fights, and also belonged to an unconditional nirvana after death if they had experienced the conditional nirvana throughout their daily living.

The principle was known as Bushido (The Bushido of the period of the civil conflict). If Samurai were to follow it in every circumstances they believed they were able to attain not only the conditional nirvana, but it also was the nirvana that is unconditional. There were four objectives of the Bushido which included (1) acceptance of death with selflessness at any time without regret or fear, (2) killing and killing selflessly in order to remove the karma of others, (3) paying respect to the honor of Samurai as well as (4) constantly being selfless.

In the following, we'll explain three steps to progress through the art of Bushido of studying Bushido as well as doing Bushido and demonstrating Bushido. Also, we will discuss his four most important values, which comprised morality, loyalty honour, courage, and loyalty throughout each phase.

Ch 2-2: First Stage: Learning Bushido

The Bushido always recommended keeping the balance that is optimal between Budo (martial art) as well as arts (cultural information) and spirituality. Thus, the purpose of learning Bushido consisted of learning Budo as well as arts as well as spirituality.

Budo was thought to be the most important ability of Samurai as they couldn't combat without mastering Budo.

The learning of Budo wasn't just to learn how to fight. It was a combination of academic and behavioural learning. Samurai believed that acquiring a proper attitudes to Budo respecting the rules, fairness and integrity of Budo and the behaviors that are associated with Budo are more significant rather than learning a few fighting skills. Samurai believed that merely learning combat techniques does not create one to become a Samurai fighter with integrity. The belief that they held was widespread in their community because they believed only Samurai who could master the behavioral aspects of Budo were able to fight selflessly and remove karma from combat.

The study of arts was essential to Samurai to develop into well-rounded individuals in order to comprehend the meanings behind fighting, death and the spiritual. The study of arts could also help open their eyes, so they had a greater and better perspective on their lives. A lot of Samurai were fond of tea ceremonies as well as Haiku-poem, music and drawing, all of which were believed to be necessary to be people who were well-rounded at the time.

The process of learning spirituality was usually based on Buddhist teachings. It was due to their religious concerns, like karma Nirvana, selflessness and eternal salvation were thoroughly taught in the Buddha's teachings. They were taught The Four Noble Truths in order to be able to understand sufferings as well as the Right practice to end suffering and karma from this world. They also studied the Noble Eightfold Path that was the guiding principle of the correct practice. To eliminate sufferings and karma, it was necessary to reaching the state of nirvana conditionally by doing selfless. They believed in particular that observing the right practice in daily living would enable their selflessness to be maintained even when fighting.

One of the largest Samurai group of warriors during the war of independence. He was extremely religious and made the decision to be the life of a Buddhist monk (The The Right Life of the Noble Eightfold Path). He refused to purchase the latest luxury items or eat expensive food items. Then, he was appointed. Also, he was well-known for his honesty and sincerity. He was not only a superb swordsman, he also was an outstanding artist. He performed Biwa (a Japanese short-necked fretted instrument) exceptionally well. He also was a well-known calligrapher and wrote beautiful Japanese poetry.

He was the most well-known adversary of Kenshin Uesugi. In the Battles of Kawanakajima was the most famous clash between the two. The man was ordained a Buddhist monk. He utilized meditation and self-reflection to improve his spirituality and strategizing plan of battle. Also, he was an outstanding calligrapher, who wrote gorgeous Japanese poetry.

At this point, Samurai minded loyalty, morality, courage and respect (LMCH later) through the following methods. Loyalty signified Samurai's devotion to Budo art, the spiritual and to their own. They believed that Budo to be the most important, as studying Budo involved learning not just strategies for fighting, but also the mindset and attitude in battle. Samurai was committed to Budo and never quit to practice this practice. They were also committed to the arts, which gave an opportunity to gain a greater understanding of Budo and spirituality as well as the the meaning behind their lives. They would get together to study or do art. They were committed to their religion so that they could be able to follow the Right Way in order to not only feel selfless and eliminate the karma that accumulated in combat for the ultimate victory to the eternal nirvana. They were also committed to themselves as the process of learning Budo as well as other arts as well as spirituality demanded a strong sense of self-reliance. Nobody could be a substitute for anyone. So, it was imperative for them to believe in themselves and therefore committed to their own self.

Morality involved Samurai's decision not give up studying Budo art, music, and even spirituality. They believed that giving up on studying these three subjects means not joining the unconditional Nirvana after the death of their loved ones. Samurais who resisted joining the unconditional nirvana could stop their peers from being able to join the unconditional nirvana due to their fighting karma. Thus, abandoning the path of study was seen as a painful and was a serious spiritual offense.

Courage was Samurai's effort to discover the meaning of both death and life through the study of Budo art, music, as well as spirituality. The spirit of courage was Samurai's determination to keep the right practice every day. Honor was the result of a successful study of Budo as well as arts and spirituality by following the right practice.

Ch 2-3: Second Stage: Practicing Bushido

Engaging in Bushido was about advancing not just techniques but also thinking and attitude towards Budo arts, Budo, as well as spirituality. As Samurai couldn't escape from their destiny, unless they decided to keep away from fighting as ordained monks and shamans, they were able to practise Budo art, music, as well as spirituality consistently with the right practice in daily routines. It was essentially similar as what Buddha was doing to attain the Nirvana conditional.

They trained in Budo predominantly through sword combat or Jujutsu. But, when they were practicing the mental and behavioral aspects of Budo the practice was done through imagery training, or meditation. In particular, meditation could aid in practicing the art of selfless combat.

The practice of arts wasn't just to enhance and broaden their horizons of living as well as death and the afterlife existence, but also to realize the sense of being selfless in different circumstances in their lives. As an example, although the tea ceremonies were very common in Zen Buddhism to experience selflessness and selflessness, it was extremely popular among Samurai to be selfless through doing selflessly cooking and drinking tea.

Samurai devoted themselves to spirituality and continued his Right Practice as it was the only way to be in a state of selflessness and reach the momentary bliss of nirvana. They constantly absorbed the wisdom and strived to achieve selflessness throughout their lives through following the method. This practice included a range of correct actions like honesty, being truthful, speaking in a manner that is correct as well as eating healthily, meditation every day, and thinking in a way that was correct.

The initial Shogun from the Muromachi Shogunate was born immediately after that of the Kamakura Shogunate. The Shogun did not fear of dying on the battlefield because his practice was sufficient to embrace any fate with a sense of selflessness. The man was well-known for his illustrations as well as his poetry.

He defeated his father, the Muromachi Shogunate and was subsequently an Shogun during the Azuchi-Momoyama Era for a short amount of time. The Shogun was well-known for his Right Practice during his everyday schedule. He was not a drinker or eat expensive food. He never broke his word. He resisted spiritual materialism to gain real enlightenment and selflessness. He kept a fair and respectful relationships with everyone. He also became famous due to his love for Japanese poetry and tea ceremonies. Particularly, he utilized tea ceremonies to help him calm to meditate, relax, and to experience a sense of selflessness. His usual practice was to take tea masters on battlefields, and also held tea ceremonies. Sen Norikyu was one of the most well-known tea masters serving him.

The family was a prosperous business family. He began learning about tea ceremonies at the age of 17 old. He worked with Nobunaga Oda as well as Hideyoshi Toyotomi (the successor to Oda) as tea master. He is the creator of "Senke School of Tea Ceremony" that has become the most renowned school for tea ceremony ever since. He was ordained as a Buddhist monk.

(Japan's most important cultural asset)

In the days before he fought in the combat against Takauji Ashikaga drafted his will, had his funeral and registered him as a deceased person in his temple. He did this because he wanted to ensure that he was able to fight the devil in the end and , consequently, fight for his selflessness.

He was a ruler in the Kyushu area. As an ordinanded Buddhist monk, he converted to a Christian in the following years. Although he was a great soldier, many accounts of his life stated that he was always averse to combat and killed. He was educated to the highest level and a well-known cultured individual. He attempted to live a the spiritual world as best possible.

Then, Samurai minded LMCH in different ways. The word loyalty means self-determination and the desire to keep practicing the correct way in their everyday life. A Right Practice was the practice of Budo art, music, as well as spirituality. It also meant trust in their levels of progress.

Morality was Samurai's dedication to keeping practice of the Right Practice correctly. Courage was the ability to enforce Samurai to continue the tradition. Honor was not just about the continuation of the practice, but also real progress in Budo, arts and religion.

Ch 2-4: Third Stage: Showing Bushido

Samurai were believed to be fearless fighters who had incredible fighting abilities. They were not just remarkable due to their exceptional capabilities and vast experience in fights, but also because of their complete learning of "dying crazy" behaviors through proper training in their everyday life for selfless combat.

So, demonstrating Bushido was the elimination of the karma of battles through engaging in selfless combat. Selfless combat was referred to as "dying crazy" in Bushido. So, fighting and living during the dying craze was doing Bushido. Dieting was considered to be the best method of combating in battle because it was how you could achieve (1) having selfless qualities, (2) being mighty as well as (3) having a hearty attitude when combat.

Like we said before, Samurai always wanted to die or even be executed without any karma, so they could attain eternal nirvana after death. Because Samurai believed that self-interest like self-interest, or a desire can create karma. Their main goal on battlefields was to fight with selflessness.

Also, they believed that selfless fights could not be a cause of karma as it doesn't cause any harm to anyone. The belief that there is no harm by selfless combat stems from the notion of "emptiness" of Buddha's lessons. According to Buddha his teachings, the most important thing that of existence is "emptiness" because it will never change. So, the only means for us to understand the emptyness is to become selfless and purify our mind by practicing the Right Way in our every day life. The reason is that purified consciousness is the emptyness. If our completely purified consciousness transformed into emptiness, we won't be able to identify the individual consciousness anymore! The emptiness of all us is the same. So, the fight between a selfless Samurai who have a pure consciousness is nothing but empty space that doesn't contain anything except eternal bliss without sufferings.

The idea of karma-free or fighting that is free of killing was utilized to justification for "taking care of oneself" or taking a suicide risk on combat to continue the spirit of selfless combat. As Samurai who have a pure and clear mind has become empty, the decision to commit suicide through the Samurai who has a pure consciousness will not differ in the same way as being killed by Samurai who had a pure consciousness. So, Samurai believed Samurai who took suicide on the battlefield would become a member of the unconditional Nirvana in the event of a selfless act of suicide.

Doing the Bushido was not only showing mercy to allies and their fellow soldiers. Particularly, their mercy included helping allies and enemies in to win their battles. But only the truly selfless Samurai were expected to have the ability to demonstrate compassion on the battlefield.

As mercy meant allow their enemies or companions to sacrifice themselves in battle that showed mercy, it was aiding suicides by those who were selfless their victims or ending their lives. Thus should Samurai trying to demonstrate mercy weren't completely selfless, doing so would cause karma to both parties. If, for instance, an Samurai was to witness someone of his allies attempt to look after his self-less actions without the proper methods to do so his kindness could aid in his suicide attempt in putting an end to the life of that person. If Samurai was able to demonstrate compassion selflessly, it will be among the most honorable actions on battlefields.

Atsumori was among Naozane's adversaries. At the time Naozane was captured, Atsumori demanded Naozane to show mercy on Samurai in killing him himself. But, Naozane could not kill the man because he was as old as his son. But, Naozane decided and killed his son while crying. In the following years, Naozane became an ordained Buddhist monk to ease his soul because Naozane did not have the courage to commit suicide and thus, caused karma to both of the two.

At this point, Samurai minded LMCH in different ways. Samurai needed to stay committed to his dying comrades regardless of the outcome. Samurai was also required to count on the loyalty of his adversaries or allies for an unselfish and free of karma fighting. A mutual commitment to the dying would build an enduring trust among both allies and enemies on battlefields. Samurai believed that loyalty to one's dying craze means being a loyal servant to the dying madness of their allies as well as enemies. In the end, as pure consciousness is essentially inertia, loyalty to the dying crazies of their allies and foes is only loyalty to one's personal dying crazy.

Morality meant ensuring a strong determination to achieve the insane in all circumstances. This commitment was crucial because it as it became the basis for friendship between the enemies and allies during battles. In addition, Samurai with the serious dedication could demonstrate their compassion to allies and foes on battlefields.

Courage is a genuine force, and will to achieve an act of selfless combat in the insanity of dying. In the case of a Samurai who were able to master both the art and the etiquette of Bushido It would be extremely difficult to remain completely selfless during certain fights. There is a chance that they would be afraid of dying, hatred towards the enemies of his, or doubts about Bushido. In these instances the fighters had to show invincible courage to sustain the dying spirit to carry on unselfish fighting.

In the end, honor was defined as an act of selfless fight. If Samurai died selflessly and their family or colleagues members would be honored. If they were to kill another Samurai in selfless ways, they'd be able to feel pride for them and their fellow Samurai. In the end, offering the mercy of a Samurai towards their allies or counterparts was extremely honorable. The honor will ultimately lead to joining the nirvana of unconditional love through unselfish, selfless and karma-free fighting.

Chapter 12: Bushido in the Era of Peace of Japan

Ch 3-1: Bushido in the Era of Peace of Japan

Since Bushido serves as a rule of Samurai's lifestyle, it is likely to be altered as the circumstances of their lives alter. A dramatic shift that they experienced in their lives occurred after the war of independence came to an end with the creation of the Tokugara regime in 1615.

The Tokugawa Family Seal

The very first Shogun in The first Shogun of the Tokugawa regime. Although he gained a lot of attention for his outstanding skills and attitude in Budo but he also was well-known for his research fascination with Confucianism, Calculus, Geometry, Pharmaceutics and Japanese tradition-based arts. The library he built was called the Suruga Library, to maintain and exchange books and reference materials on various subjects.

The powerful regime of arms might finally be able to control every clan as a central government. With this new time of peace Samurai will not be on battlefields any more to expand their territories.

The Tokugawa regime introduced a different class system, which Samurai were the top level. There were a variety of ranks within the Samurai class, based on territorial size, blood ties to the Tokugawa family members, alliances to the Tokugawa family members on battlefields or the history and fame of names from families. The new rulers gave Samurai different positions and tasks in accordance with their ranks. Because the structure of class was set and Samurai were given specific jobs under the Tokugawa clans and the regimes and clans, the majority of Samurai changed into white collars and be paid by either Tokugawa clan leaders or family members. Because they remained at certain ranks, with a specific levels of work and responsibilities, it was only natural for them to begin to make a an effort to preserve their specific lifestyles that their children would inherit. In the meantime, Samurai, especially, the rulers required a new Bushido to rule Samurai into the modern era of peace.

But, even if Bushido during the time of civil war was no longer appropriate to the Tokugawa regime It was never wise to Tokugawa to instantly deny the fundamentals of Bushido. The reason for this was that the spirit of the bushido was still revered by the Samurai brain. So, Tokugawa started adding more theories to the essence in order that Samurai could naturally adopt more proper Bushido during the time of peace.

The principal reason for adding the interpretation of the present was to replace individualism in the previous Bushido by hierarchical collectivism. This meant total respect of the clan head towards Tokugawa. Tokugawa regime. Thus, the collectiveism to be a Samurai within a clan was total obedience by Samurai families towards the clan's leader. In the end the Samurai was required to follow the rules of his family. That is when one Samurai family member didn't be obedient, it was interpreted as a sign that all his family didn't show conformity.

The new meaning of the definition of dying insane did not have to be selfless in fighting instead of dying in the name of clans, families as well as families, clans and the Tokugawa family (the the rulers in this case). The Samurai was required to be willing to die when ruling class expected them to be dead in order to demonstrate loyalty, forgiveness or innocence. So, the modern Bushido at the time of peace demanded Samurai to remain in their dying because they needed to commit suicide at the request from their rulers.

Finally it was the Tokugawa administration reaffirmed the understandings of the core of the ancient Bushido by introducing the aesthetics of formalism and aesthetics to it. Values and meanings of dying in death and LMCH were reformulated and redefined in accordance with aesthetics and formality. The Bushido at the time of peace became widely recognized in the following years as the normative Bushido of Japan in famous novels like "Hagakure" by Tsunetomo Yamamoto as well as "Bushiso, the Soul of Japan" by Inazo Nitobe.

Although there are a variety of distinctions between the older and the new Bushido The most notable change was the primary issue of Bushido. The Bushido during the time of civil war was focused on a single Samurai that had to remain until death, sacrificing his life for combat through the dying of a madman. However the Bushido during the time of peace focused on ruling class through the sacrifice of a single Samurai. The virtues of sacrifice in the modern Bushido allowed the ruling class to contain the anger of unsatisfied Samurai over a period of more than two hundred years. Tokugawa's desire to introduce fresh interpretations to the spirit of the traditional Bushido to govern the Samurai class was achieved effectively.

In the Bushido in the time of peace Samurai were awed by LMCH through the following methods. Their loyalty was strictly for the ruling class. Their morality was unending and complete dedication to their kings. If they didn't adhere to the moral code, they'd be disqualified from performing Harakiri (Seppuku). Furthermore, the head of the clan could terminate the name of his family. If the clan was found to have committed a crime against morality or the law, the Tokugawa regime was able to terminate the clan. If this was the case, Samurai from the clan would have to be unemployed and/or Ronin (masterless Samurai). Like you've seen here, because ignoring morals could end the life of a Samurai as well, the clan's heads as well as family masters were required to watch their followers with great care. Alongside this effort to teach their followers to practice Bushido during the time of peace in order to train their members into submitting to.

It was usually the Samurai's perseverance. Samurai were required to serve authorities regardless of their beliefs or values and even their conscience. They were sometimes forced to remain courageous and intolerant to the point of being unreasonable and adhere to the moral code.

Samurai believed that they could earn honour due to the dedication and perseverance and actions that reflected the moral code, loyalty, and bravery. Particularly the honor of an Samurai to preserve their family's names as well as loyalty to the clan's head. Transferring family names down to generation after generation was a very noble act for a Samurai. Thus, living a long and peaceful life was regarded as an honorable act during the time of peace. It is no surprise that killing for ruling class was regarded as a noble act.

Ch 3 the question is: how did The Bushido in the Era of Peace evolved into to be the Standard Bushido?

The idea is that two books created Bushido in the time of peace into the norm Bushido. The first, Hagakure, was written by Tsunetomo Yamamoto. It was released around 100 years before the Tokugawa administration began. The rulers especially embraced the book for its emphasis on an unwavering devotion to their leaders through unending perseverance and self-sacrifice by a single Samurai. The book was regarded as the standard of Bushido at the time of peace.

According to Hagakure that the Bushido during the time of peace was actually the means of dying. The death was always the central theme in Bushido but Hagakure's real meaning was death as a way to die for the ruling class. The selfless fight against the insane battlefields wasn't thought of and was not valued anymore.

Hagakure highlighted the honorable death of Samurai. Honorable deaths were celebrated with the formality and elegance of Samurai's self sacrifice. They were willing and calm to consent to "ordered" or "responsible" death as a sign of their loyalty and respect for the leaders. Instead of waiting to fight for their lives to be saved They had to remain through death in order to prepare to face the formal and beautiful dying in their honor.

Hagakure celebrated the Bushido in the age of peace. He added the elegance and formality of self-sacrifice, with a nostalgia of the Bushido during the time of the civil war. Indeed, Samurai in the Tokugawa regime, including the author of it, Tsunetomo, tended to be awed by such nostalgia-inducing cuteness.

For Tsunetomo the reason he favored the nostalgia-inducing charm came directly from his own experience as the son of a Samurai. His birthplace was in the Samurai household in the year 1659. The family was not blessed with physical health, so he could be unable to practice Budo in a very effective way. He did however, practiced martial the arts to become a competent bureaucrat in the Saga-clan. As there was no war during the time of peace so he was not required to endure the pain of those who were dying in battle. But, since there was no time of no battles, his cuteness towards the Bushido during the time of civil war was so compelling that he began to justify his life during the time of peace using the ethos of the Bushido in the period that was civil war. The concept he came up with was the new structure for LMCH. It was in a way similar with the one we discussed in Chapter 3 of the book.

The book that followed, Bushido, was published around 32 years following the Tokugawa regime was over. The book was a stylization of the Bushido that was popular during the time of peace. It was published by English written by Inazo Nitobe. The book was later translated into other languages, such as Japanese. It was regarded as the first and largest guide to Japanese Bushido. Many non-Japanese scholars analyzed the book in order to come up with diverse conceptual frameworks and concepts for Japanese Bushido. Japanese Bushido. In the end, a lot of Japanese have learned about the Bushido through the book.

According to the writer, Inazo Nitobe claims that the Japanese Bushido was built on respect for Samurai and a loyalty to rulers. Samurai showed their loyalty by dying as well as self-sacrificing for their rulers. The willingness to demonstrate the loyalty of a person was considered to be very noble and living with honour became the primary purpose of the Samurai's existence. Although his concept of Bushido is very much like the one of Hagakure He emphasized more on the aesthetics of honor and loyalty.

Ch 3-3: Musashi Miyamoto's Bushido in the Era of Peace

It is no surprise that in the early days of the Tokugawa Shogunate, there were numerous Samurai warriors still living within the Bushido that was the time of civil conflict. Because they were a dying breed and maintained their independence and dedication to fighting for their lives without fear of becoming madness, a variety of changes to the Bushido that came with the time of peace frightened and dissatisfied the Samurai. Apart from the disappointments and confusions They eventually came to the realization that they weren't necessary and appropriate for the ruling class in the current era.

One of the older Samurai of the present day included Musashi Miyamoto who was approximately 25 when the Tokugawa government was established. He was not only one of the top martial artists in Japan however, he was also an extremely well-known musician and spiritualist. Particularly, his art was extraordinary and it is possible to see the paintings of his as important Cultural Properties of Japan. Even though he had the potential to be an excellent monk due to his incredible spirituality and understanding of Buddhist teachings but he opted not to become orally ordained. The decision was based on the belief of his that being the monk didn't mean dying and thus, wasn't the ideal way to be a master of dying insane to self-sacrificing fighting and death.

He wrote a five volumes in order to convey his thoughts on Bushido as it was in the present. According to the book Gorinsho, Bushido was the basis of the Samurai's lifestyle for making them more superior in art, Budo, as well as spirituality. He also questioned the formality and beauty of the Samurai's demise in the modern Bushido. He argued that formality and aesthetics shouldn't be over stressed and valued. Instead, focus on the true value of death must be emphasized. Death's real significance is in its significance as an important moment in life that allowed us to enter the eternal bliss of nirvana. If Samurai concentrated too much on aesthetics and formality it would be difficult to appreciate the significance and value of dying. Since everyone dies one day, Samurai still had to be alive and live completely for the nirvana that is unconditional regardless of battles or there were battles or.

Chapter 13: Buddhism Spirituality in the Bushido of the Era of Civil War

Buddhism is a popular form of spirituality as a part of the Bushido during the time of civil conflict. This is due to the fact that Samurai as well as Buddha were both influenced by the same fundamental aspects of spirituality, such as the sufferings of selflessness, selflessness, such as karma, and the Nirvana. Thus, it was sensible to Samurai to take lessons from Buddha and practice selfless fight in order to attain the nirvana of unconditional love.

Typically, studying Buddha's teachings was understanding The Four Noble Truths. In order to learn Buddha's practices (The right practice) was about learning and implementing what is known as the Noble Eightfold Path. They were the foundation of spirituality in Bushido.

Ch 4-1: The Bushido of the Era of Civil War and the Four Noble Truths

The reality about suffering, reality of the causes that cause suffering, the reality of ending suffering as well as the factual ways to stop suffering constitute the four Noble Truths. The first Buddha teaching focused on The Four Noble Truths.

In the context of suffering, having sufferings is a natural part of life. Also there is always some thing or someone that causes people feel unhappy, anxious sad, angry, or depressed. So, the initial step toward achieving the ultimate bliss was to accept the reality of the various afflictions that we experience throughout our lives.

For Samurai the fates of their combatants brought about serious pain including being murdered, preparing to be killed and even living with death. The process of learning the Bushido during the time of war was started by observing the hardships they endured in their own lives. They would then learn to accept their sufferings.

Based on the reality of reasons for suffering, our desire for material things are the cause of suffering. We are driven by money to earn as much as we are able to. We would like to stay physically and mentally young for the rest of our lives. This will cause suffering in the event that we are unable to satisfy these desire. We will never be able to fully fulfill any desire by any means as there are ever-changing desires.

Samurai had a variety of desires that could cause different pains. They were determined to prevail regardless of the odds, to invade in order to expand their territories or defeat fear of death when fighting. In all likelihood they wanted to not to lose their lives in battles. This was believed to be the root of pain, such as losing battles, getting killed or losing their territory, or fearing the death of a soldier in battle. Samurai was also convinced that such troubles would lead to another for a lifetime. Because these wants would hinder the dying and those who are dying of fighting for their lives and fight for their lives, they believed that they would never attain the nirvana of unconditional love in the event that they were unable to get rid of their needs.

Based on the real factors that cause suffering, the initial way to end suffering is discern between sufferer-free and the ones that are causing suffering. Thus, Samurai tried to understand and understand their needs in a way that was accurate. After that, they thought about whether their desires caused pain and suffering to discover ways to manage their desires.

Based on the factual basis of a sigh-free life, controlling your own desires can eliminate pain. Although it's one of the most important truths, it is essential to be extremely careful and observant to fully grasp the meaning of a cessation of suffering. In particular, it is imperative to remember that Buddha didn't tell us to sever our desire totally. He instead advised us to only eliminate suffering-causing desires.

In this case, for instance, your need to make money in order to provide for your family members will not result in pain as long as your need is satisfied through earning enough money to feed your family. If you want to make more funds will begin to cause pain. It is due to the fact that your desire to earn more money won't last all the time.

For Samurai the desire to win fights was not a cause for suffering so long as they knew what winning really meant. To truly win a fight the only thing they needed to do was battle through the dying insane. What really won, then wasn't about executing or getting killed, but ending the battle karma to be a part of the eternal nirvana. Therefore, both the Samurai as well as his counterpart would really win if they worked in a way that was selflessly.

In accordance with the true nature of the path that leads to the cessation of suffering The Right Practice that is taught by Buddha is the sole method that can control the desires, and thus alleviate suffering. Buddha was the teacher of The Noble Eightfold Path as the basis of right practice. Thus, Samurai constructed their own version of the Noble Eightfold Path into the Bushido to ensure that they continue with the Right Practice correctly in their every day practices.

Ch 4-2: The Bushido of the Era of Civil War and the Noble Eightfold Path

The Noble Eightfold Path (the path which follows) is the guiding principle of the right practice of Buddha. Buddha created his path on the basis of his own experience of the practices. Buddha was confident that those who was sincerely committed to the path through the practice could be in a position to cleanse their mind to remain selfless in pursuit of the unending Nirvana.

"Right View" means correct knowledge in the Four Noble Truths. It was extremely vital at the time Samurai took up the art of Bushido. It was due to the fact that it was impossible to know the meaning of battle without fully understanding the fundamentals. The right perspective could help educate Samurai who lived in the grave.

"Right Intention" means one's acceptance and acknowledgement in the Four Noble Truths in daily everyday life. Also"Right Intention" means that"Right Practice" or Right Practice begins with correctly knowing and comprehending The Four Noble Truths.

The right attitude will let Samurai to comprehend how important it is to be selfless. Death offered them the opportunity not only to give up their lives, but to accept and accept the truth in whatever circumstances. Samurai were required to sustain the highest level of progress in the pursuit of the ideal goal to be selfless in battles.

"Right Effort" means making honest efforts to adhere to the right behavior in all situations. It is impossible to last without a second path, "Right Livelihood", which is to try to sustain the religious life as an ordinated monk at any time. In the case of Samurai this was to maintain with the Right Practice with spiritual mindset and an attitude that resembles monks at all times.

Buddha employed "Right Speech", "Right Action", "Right Mindfulness" along with "Right Concentration" to explain how to make the best effort in greater specific terms. A good speech is being attentive to the content of the speech, its words, their timing phrases, meanings, and purpose that you are expressing in your talk. If you fail to take note of the spiritual significance of the speech you are giving, you can cause karma and harm the other audience members. In the example above, if there are 10 people who listen to your speech, all of the viewers would have their own unique way to interpret the speech. Samurai were trained to be fair, honest moral and faithful in order that the words they spoke could not be interpreted as karma.

A righteous action is a way of maintaining the right behavior and philosophies. A righteous action is typically described as the five commands of Buddhism and include "Do not kill", Don't take anything", "Do not drink alcohol", "Do not get involved in sexual activities that are not ethical" And "Do not give into the temptation of the spiritual materialism."

You will notice that "Do not kill" seems to be a bit contradictory for Samurai as their goal was to battle on the battlefield. But, they didn't believe it was in contradiction at any point. It was due to the fact that they considered that killing could be free of karma if it happened as a outcome of selfless combat on the battlefield. So, the sole requirement for a karma-free death was that each Samurai and his comrade will fight for their lives without fear of becoming in a state of madness. The reason for this was that an attitude of selflessness throughout the entire process was so crucial for Samurai.

The term "righteous mindfulness" had two definitions: spiritual tolerance as well as ability to differentiate positive and negative desires. If you possess the ability to discern good from bad tolerance, then you'll have the ability to see all things around you and embrace these things without prejudgment either because of personal needs or individual preference. Samurai sought to understand the Buddha's wisdom, truths and beauty in their lives and the true meaning of living in the end as well as the power of mercy as well as selfless living and possibility of achieving nirvana in a conditional manner by being open to all situations.